I0015150

Small-Business Entrepreneurship:

Stories of Grit, Risk, and Reward from Startup to Success

Allan Woolway

Copyright © 2019 Allan Woolway

All rights reserved.

ISBN: 978-1-7335990-0-9

PREFACE

This book shows what it means to have grit as an entrepreneur. It covers an in-depth history of how one person handled many different opportunities and business situations during an ever-changing career. Later, it offers stories of other entrepreneurs and their own journeys whether it be through success or failure.

Many of the stories in the book focus on the technology industry, since that is where I spent most of my career, but there are also stories of restaurants, sports gear, logistics management, warehousing, and more. Real world examples offer rich, engaging opportunities to learn from those who've gone before you. Treat this book, and our stories, as a learning tool as you embark on your own career journeys.

Enjoy the book, learn by example, and if you have questions email us or join our online community.

www.smallbusinessentrepreneurship.com

Table of Contents

Introduction:
Staying in the Game as a Serial Entrepreneur

Entrepreneurial spirit is not something that can be taught — but it can be shared, trained, and groomed. Likewise, grit isn't an attitude you can adopt from scratch, but it is something you can bring out in yourself.

Grit is based on an individual's ability to focus on something with passion and determination. It is built around a powerful motivation that compels you to overcome obstacles or challenges that lay ahead. Most successful entrepreneurs, athletes, musicians, and many others have grit.

The reason for discussing both grit and entrepreneurship in the same breath is that you absolutely need grit to be a successful entrepreneur. You need strong intrinsic motivation, the ability to push and work hard, and a very high tolerance for risk. To some extent, these characteristics are innate. Many of the entrepreneurs described in this book (including the author) demonstrated grit, determination, and even stubbornness at a young age.

But grit and the entrepreneurial spirit can be fostered, refined, and strengthened. Working with mentors, reading books such as this, and networking with peers can help develop your entrepreneurial skills. First, of course, you must decide if you want to take the risks and make the sacrifices that it takes to be a successful entrepreneur. And once you've taken the leap and started your own business, do you have what it takes to stay in the game?

What does it take to be a successful entrepreneur?

So you have an idea for a product or a service, and you're considering whether to start a business. In order to make that decision, you need to assess the viability of your idea. This is a business choice: can your idea be the basis for a profitable business? At the same time, you need to assess your own attitudes. Do you have the drive and determination to push your idea to success?

To assess the viability of your idea, you need to start asking questions like the following:

- Is there a market for your idea? How big is the market, how reachable is it, and what are people willing to pay?
- What alternatives do your prospective customers have? It is important to understand your competitive landscape and recognize that people may choose to "do nothing" instead of purchasing your product if it is not necessary.
- Is your idea original and could it potentially be patentable?
- How will your idea become a business — that is, what will be necessary to run the business and how will you make money?
- What is the right timing for launching your idea?

Additionally, you need to evaluate your own attitudes and the practical necessities of your life. Even if you have a great idea, starting a business without thoroughly and honestly answering these questions is a recipe for failure:

- Can you afford the risk of working full time on your new business? Often, entrepreneurs stay in their current jobs so there is less risk involved while starting a new venture. On the other hand, working another job means less time and energy to devote to your idea.
- If you start a business and don't make any income for 6–18 months (which is typical), can you live on your savings, on another income in the family, or on borrowed money? You must have an answer for these questions before taking the leap.
- How important is your personal life? If you have a partner, family, or children, you will need to consider the sacrifices they will make as you start your business. Employees might leave at 5 p.m., but entrepreneurs stay and continue working, to either get the sale or to solve a problem. If there is a choice of getting a quote to a prospective client the next morning or going out to dinner and having some drinks, the decision should be easy. And if that

mindset doesn't sound like a fit, perhaps entrepreneurship isn't for you.

There is a basic rule that if you are going into business, you will need at least enough capital to last a year especially if you do not have any other source of income coming into the household. If you are an individual consultant with no overhead, then all income you make can potentially be used for the cost of living. But if you have an office and a few employees, then they need to be paid, overhead costs and taxes need to be covered, and you will only be paid if there is a profit. This might sound easy, but it's not!

The most reliable advice I give to new entrepreneurs is to work with mentors. Learn from others who have experienced being in businesses like yours. Learn from others whose leadership, style, or success you admire. Learn from stories of successful companies of all sizes. And learn from books like this, that present simple, real-world examples of what a serial entrepreneur can face over the course of a career.

When starting a business, you make the most progress when you work on the edge of your comfort zone. You'll be pushing yourself, taking risks, and working very hard. If that sounds intimidating, you may want to stick to a more conventional job. If that sounds like an exciting challenge, congratulations!

> **What is success to you? You must define success for yourself or you will never know when you have reached your goal.**

You have grit and the entrepreneurial spirit, and once you have the right idea you'll be ready to build your own business.

Part 1:

My Journey in Grit and Entrepreneurship

Chapter 1:
What Does Grit Have to Do with Push-ups?

To have grit, you need passion and determination. For me, those characteristics didn't show up until I was 15. Though I had never been good at sports, that year I developed an athletic pursuit that turned into an obsession and started to teach me that I have grit.

DO YOU HAVE GRIT? HOW WOULD YOU KNOW?

Prior to 1964 I was usually the last kid picked for any team sport. I was just not very popular, fast, or athletic. In 1964 just before turning 15, I saw gymnastics on TV for the first time. I was immediately drawn to it, so I went to the library and did some research. I found out that strength was the starting point for all gymnastics, so I started doing push-ups and pull-ups in my basement. It was nothing drastic yet, just consistently working out, every day.

At the same time, to learn more about my hobby I started reading strength magazines. During the winter of 1963–64, I read that the world record for push-ups was 1,687 in an hour and a half. As soon as I read that, I thought I could attempt to beat the record. A passion was born, and I started working out harder every day.

In the summer of 1964, I was a lifeguard at a camp in the Catskills Mountains of New York. Two of the camp counselors ran a gym in New York City. I told them of my goal. They were skeptical, but they agreed that if I wanted to try they would set up an official way to test the record.

Another counselor at the camp was named Angelo. He had an eye-catching physique — strong, lean, and very muscular. I looked strong, but not like Angelo. He heard about my planned record attempt and decided to try for the record at the same time as me.

I worked out every day doing push-ups, dips between chairs, and pull-ups. I did hundreds and hundreds every day. Passion and determination were starting to manifest in my behavior.

The attempt date was August 2, 1964. Witnesses were on hand. The gym owners took over a bungalow that had four rooms. Angelo would be in one room and I would be in another, each with a team of people counting and tracking the push-ups. It was a hot summer day, with no air conditioning.

Prior to August 2, I had determined a plan. To manage the ninety minutes, I would do 20 push-ups each minute: ten when the clock's second hand hit 12 and ten more when it hit 6. At that rate, I could do 1,800 in two hours. Angelo had his own plan.

The clock started. I did ten push-ups. The form had to be perfect to count: chest to the ground, elbows straight. Of course, the first ten were easy. When the clock hit the six, I pumped out another ten. After 20 minutes, I was still on track. The only problem was sweat. On that hot and humid day, there was so much sweat that even drying the floor could not keep my arms from slipping.

Soon a solution presented itself. Thirty minutes into the contest, Angelo gave up. From that point on, during the time between completing one set and starting the next, I would run to the next room with a dry floor. It was crazy, but it worked.

> Why was I able to unofficially break the world record? Was I that strong? No, what I had that day was grit. I overcame exhaustion, heat, and wet floors. Could someone else have broken that record? Of course. But no one had as much determination as me on that day in 1964.

An hour in, I was still on schedule. All five observers were counting and waiting for me to run out of steam. Campers crammed the windows looking in to see Allan doing push-ups and going for the record.

Eighty minutes in, I knew I could do it. How could I squeeze out a few more? I added an extra push-up to any set where I could manage it: nothing dramatic, just enough to ensure I would break 1,800. When the clock hit 90 minutes, I was up to 1,810 push-ups.

The room exploded; everyone was happy. I just sat on the floor for a few minutes, soaked in sweat. The gym owners made a notarized plaque for me with every signature on it. I still have it.

Is reaching a goal the end or the beginning? The

> Dreams without goals are just dreams, and they ultimately fail. To make a goal you must apply discipline and determination. Don't confuse movement with progress. Without taking risk, nothing worthwhile will be accomplished.

feeling of breaking that record, and achieving a difficult goal was addictive. I now knew that a sound plan and intense training could help me build the grit needed to overcome the odds. Now that I realized dreams could be fulfilled, I wanted to continue to build upon this experience.

Every summer we had color wars at camp: the camp was split in half and we competed in all sports, from swimming to volleyball, softball, and track events. I used to practice underwater swimming (completely underwater, no splashing of any kind). I practiced holding my breath. In fact, I used to practice holding my breath in Spanish class getting ready for the summer.

This summer it was time for the underwater swim competition. I knew inside that I had to win. We had an Olympic-size pool and I had been able to go 1.5 times the length of the pool on one breath. I had one main competitor who was older and bigger than me. Luckily because my last name starts with "W" I got to go last. The best anyone did prior to me that year in our Olympic-size pool was about 1.3 laps.

I said to myself "I am going to kill this." I took a bunch of deep breaths to get my oxygen level up, and I was under the water. I went to the end and kicked off to come back. I passed the 1/3 marker where the other competitor quit.

I kept going.

My lungs were contracting and expanding trying to get oxygen. I fought it, trying to not let any air out. I made it to the end of the pool. I was entirely spent. All I could do was raise my arm. If two people had not lifted me out, I could have drowned.

I was not the best swimmer in the world, not even close, but I pushed harder than I ever had and met my goal. If I did not have grit, I would have definitely quit at 1.5 times the length of the pool when my lungs were screaming at me to breathe.

> A necessary characteristic of an entrepreneur is that strong desire to "win."

I fought the spasms in my diaphragm and set the wall as my goal. Did I think about possibly drowning because I had nothing left? No. I just knew what I had to do. Thank you to the two counselors who pulled me out of the water.

BUILDING ON MY DISCOVERED GRIT

Once summer camp was over, I knew I had grit. I had come to recognize the feelings of passion and determination, and I could tell what it would feel like to apply those traits to the rest of my life. I felt like I could be good at anything I set my mind to. At this point in life, I chose gymnastics. I found my passion and had the grit to push myself beyond most limits of sanity.

The only problem with my gymnastics dream was that we had no coach at my high school. No problem; I found gymnastics on TV and watched carefully. I took out a book from the library.

I decided that getting stronger was a necessity, so I came up with a plan. We had one gym in the school. I found out I was not allowed to use the gym until the sports teams were done with practice. The parallel bars and horse were in a janitor closet with very tall ceilings. So, I asked the janitor if I could work out in his closet until the gym was empty every day. He said ok. (Remember this was 1964–65, and there were not as many laws about child safety as there are now — having a student work out in a closet on the parallel bars and horse with no spotter and no coach could never happen today!)

I would close myself in the gym storage closet from 3:00 to 4:45. Then I would leave the closet and go out to the empty gym and work on the rings and high bar, again with no spotter or training. I did this until 6 p.m. Then I walked home, ate dinner and by 7 p.m. I was in the basement for the rest of my workout.

I decided that since I could do 20 push-ups a minute I should incorporate that into my workout. So, from 7 to 8 p.m. I would do 1,000 push-ups. Then from 8 to 10 p.m., I would do 600 pull-ups and 600 dips. For dips I used tall backs of chairs facing back to back, which meant I needed to control the chairs from not squeezing together while doing the dips. That made it much harder — knees to the floor and all the way up.

I did my whole workout in a similar fashion to the push-up record. I would do 10 dips, then 10 pull-ups. Then dips, then pull-ups. The difference was that I did one set per minute of the dips and pull-ups — 120 minutes, 1,200 reps. Then from 10 to 11 p.m. I would use a few weights for some different muscle groups and practice my one-handed handstands on the floor. This workout was from Monday to Friday, every day. On Tuesdays, I would have a friend come over, and I would practice doing pull-ups with him on my back (we each weighed 155lbs) then practice doing push-ups with him on my back. This was fun and challenging. Think of it as a strength day.

I definitely had the grit to endure, by myself, with no external motivating factors. My internal motivation and determination were enough.

The passion I had for getting stronger was so great that I used to do more exercises while in class. In Spanish I practiced holding my breath; in Social Studies I held myself off the chair with my arms. The only thing I thought about was getting stronger and having more stamina.

This is all that I remember from high school. Academically I was in college prep and did average, partially because I did not have time to study. I ended up going to a state college with no gymnastics team.

While working out in the gym, I had one too many falls and injured two disks in my spine. I lived with the pain until 1975, when I finally had the bad disks removed. Once my back was hurt, I had to give up gymnastics. But I never gave up working out; I just reduced it to one hour a day of strength exercises.

> There are many more examples of grit found in stories of other entrepreneurs later in this book.

Gymnastics taught me that, even without external motivation or external reward, I could demonstrate grit.

THE CAR PASSION

My next passion was cars. I needed to earn money while in college and went to work at a Sunoco gas station, pumping gas. (In New Jersey gas must be pumped for you by an attendant — no self-serve.) I happened to get a job at a station that had a wonderful, smart mechanic. He was a great influence on me because I learned that reading technical books about cars gave you an edge over other mechanics who did not do the same. He was a mechanic who worked on high-performance race cars (mostly street racers). This got me interested in race cars.

With my interest piqued, my competitive gene became active again. So, while going to college full time, I started working 30–35 hours a week at the gas station. I wanted to race.

I purchased a 1960 Pontiac Bonneville with a 389 cubic inch engine, 4 speed and tri-power (3 two-barrel carburetors). This was great: off to the drag races. I was hooked. School became secondary. I raced every Sunday and sometimes on Saturday also — all on a strict budget. I

> **Whenever possible learn from someone who has more experience and is willing to be your mentor.**

worked even more hours, every holiday, Christmas, Easter, and New Year's. I worked out a commission for every quart of oil or windshield washer fluid I sold. Customers loved me because when they came in for gas I would check the oil, transmission fluid, windshield washer fluid and fill up anything they needed. I even washed the windows of every car, making commissions and getting tips (especially on holidays and during the gas shortage).

I had the added benefit of learning about tuning a car from an expert, who owned the service station. I decided to start my own side business of tuning and detailing cars. I then purchased every book I could about tuning foreign cars because they gave mechanics a lot of trouble (especially side-draft carburetors). I became knowledgeable at foreign car tune-ups. I graduated from college and became a teacher. While teaching I was growing the auto detailing and tune-up business.

I had a one-bay garage under my apartment. One wall was lined with tune-up kits that I purchased when on sale at different department stores. This was back in the day of spark plugs, points, rotors and caps, side draft carburetors, two and four-barrel carburetors. I had an instant set of customers: the teachers in my school, their relatives, and their friends. I used to get a period off and lunch during the day. I could be found outside tuning a car or taking a customer's car a block away to wash and wax. I was fast and good at it. My problem was working outside in the cold and the physical nature of the business was not the best suited for my future. I still had the backup of being a teacher.

During this period, I decided to try something other than car tune-ups and detailing. I also stopped drag racing, since my back was not totally healed yet.

Chapter 2:
Taking the Dive Into a New Business

A HOBBY STORE BUSINESS:

I decided to give my body a break from the heavier physical work that cars needed. I found a hobby that in turn, led me to the second step in the life of a serial entrepreneur. Little did I know that even more grit would be required to hold down a full-time teaching position while trying to make it in the retail world.

I found a new obsession: radio-controlled (RC) race cars. I enjoyed the sport of racing RC Cars and meeting an entirely new group of friends. Most people in this sport did not have a lot of spare money, but they spent almost all of it on their radio-controlled cars and planes. To me, this felt like an opportunity. I thought that if more people could find out about racing these radio-controlled cars, a larger business could be created.

Even at this early stage, I believed I could learn about the business and be successful. This is a crucial component of being an entrepreneur and a very important part of any business. If you think there is a great chance you will not succeed, then don't start (evaluating your risk tolerance is a key factor here). You must assume that you can be successful and do better than your competitors (find out who your customer base will be prior to starting). With that foundational assumption, you just need to find out how to get to that goal. You must be flexible, open to learning from others, and ready to change directions at any time — but with a strong belief in yourself and your ability.

In 1977 I decided to turn my hobby into a business by starting a small hobby store selling remote control race cars and airplanes. The first thing I did was to travel to all the hobby stores in the same business within a 75-mile radius. I observed what they did, who they were, and who their customers were.

Importantly, I did all of this while I kept teaching so that I had money to live and invest. That was an important, and good, strategic choice. At the same time, I made a few mistakes in evaluating the business proposition. I

> Starting part time allows your business to grow gradually while relying on the income and benefits from your full-time job.

learned that the customer base was not large, which should have been a red flag. I noticed that customers overall had a real budget issue and had to purchase new parts when money was available, which should have been another red flag. This was a sport (hobby), not a necessity. Nevertheless, I thought that if I built a store, created a track to hold events, and was good at building and tuning these radio-controlled cars and planes, then people would come and I would have a profitable business.

Ultimately, despite the red flags that came up in my research, I decided to open a store. I was young, inexperienced and did not have a mentor to talk with about whether this was a viable business.

> **If something does not feel right, take another look before investing your resources and losing valuable time and money.**

I found a small retail space that was a converted garage with a large picture window, nice entrance, and a place to hang a sign. The store was on a side street across from a large train station. This store was not in the best retail location (This will turn out to be a problem).

I signed a contract for renting the store. I ran the store after school and on the weekends. I continued teaching so that I could wait for the business to build and create a profit. I did not want the business to fail because I ran out of money. This was a good decision: having enough money to invest in the business (and enough to live on meanwhile!) was crucial to my success.

Through all these hardships, I continued to push, believing I could succeed. But after a year of losing weight and little sleep, I made the decision to close the Hobby Shop, sell my inventory at a loss and look for some other business that would earn more money. I still believed that I could succeed — I just needed a different venue.

What did I learn from this experience? I did not make the classic mistake of quitting my original job (I kept teaching), which earned the money to support the startup. The startup would not have done better working full time, since my customers either came after school, after work, or on the weekend.

What I really learned was the importance of understanding your customer base. I learned that I did not want to be in a business where I had to rely on hobbyists to make my living. Many hobbyists had very little money or just came to talk and look. I wanted to make sure that the next business I would start had a larger customer base, one that needed my services or products, not just as a hobby.

TRY AND TRY AGAIN

I tried several other small businesses in the following years, but none of them fit my passion. For example, I tried my hand at a lawn mower repair shop. It was a lot of physical work, dirty, and not rewarding at all. If you fixed a lawn mower, there was very little money to make, and customers were just getting them fixed because they weren't running correctly. There

> **At some point in life you will fail. If you don't fail, you are not even trying. To get something that you never had, you need to do something you never did. Be open to and assess the risk, then make your decision.**

was no fun in this, like there had been in race cars. I needed fun for part of my motivation, so I moved on.

Since I always belonged to a gym and loved going to the gym, I considered owning my own gym. I decided to take a part-time job working at a local health club as a trainer. Most trainers took people through their first one or two sessions. They would greet people and clean the equipment. But since I had been in sports and had coached gymnastics and cross-country as a teacher, I already liked making a difference. So, I followed people and their workouts for a long time. I used to hold special strength training sessions for professionals at 9 p.m. after the gym closed so that we could have privacy and not wait for machines. I enjoyed it when these adults made progress.

This was fun for me, and the work itself was a fit for my passion and skills. However, after getting to understand what it takes to get customers, payments, and the business side of things to function smoothly, I was not as excited about owning a gym. Employees also make a difference: in a gym, they would normally be your biggest problem and biggest expense. The majority of other "trainers" that worked at the gym did not really enjoy working out themselves, so helping whenever they had free time was not on their list of things to do (many just wanted to socialize). I did come to realize here that there is a percentage of employees that will follow the lead and do a better, more dedicated job, if someone there is also caring and working to support clients. So, I decided to keep looking for that next passion, which could be translated into a new direction for my life. That passion did not turn into opening a gym.

But I had learned about passion, about fun, about the importance of knowing your customers and employees, and of course, I had learned even more about what it takes to become a successful entrepreneur.

DISCOVERING THE MAGIC OF COMPUTERS

In December of 1981, I was still teaching middle school science. Many lessons were based around simulations of what physically happened on the earth and in the universe. Some of these simulations would involve moving all the desks and chairs in the room to make space for creating a mock solar system. One simulation that I made every year was that of the moon going around the earth as the earth travels around the sun. It was cool to see how the moon must revolve and rotate a specific way. Then in class we would plot out the path of the moon relative to the sun. It was a very interesting simulation. The students really enjoyed it, and it helped them visualize and understand the science.

The school had decided that it was going to purchase computers for running programs for the classroom to assist in math, reading, and science classes at the elementary and middle school level. Since many of the teachers (including myself) had never touched a computer, it was decided that taking a class at the local Radio Shack was a good idea. So I signed up for the class along with about eight other math and science teachers.

Many of the Radio Shack stores back then had classrooms set up with TSR-80 computers. These were non-graphical black and white screens. The course we were interested in was basic programming. On the first night we were introduced to the computer and what some of the capabilities were with the basic programming language. It immediately struck a chord with me. "Wow, this is really cool." I asked the instructor, "You mean, if I want to develop a program to simulate a formula for comparing the speed of planet rotation, I could do that?" I was told, YES.

I decided this was worth looking into, so I purchased every programming book relating to running "Basic on the Tandy" that was available on the shelf before leaving the store that night. I went home and started reading the books, striving to understand the sample programs in each.

I decided that the next day after school I would go to a Radio Shack to type in some of the sample programs to see what they would do. I told the salesman I was thinking about purchasing the computer, but I really just wanted to try it out. Guess what, the programs I typed in worked! This basic programming language did not look that tough, and I was already visualizing what I could do with such a powerful tool.

The first thing I did was to write some simple math programs. Then counter programs. I wondered if I could make that little box move across the screen. If I could, that might open a door to a simulation.

This was the start of another passion, another obsession, and another chance to exercise my grit and determination. Every night I would write programs until 1 a.m. I would teach during the day (writing more programs during free periods), then go to a different Radio Shack at night. I couldn't keep going back to the same Radio Shack, because they really wanted to sell computers, not have someone learn on them (except in the school-sponsored class that we were paying for). By the second week of the class, I was already beyond the teacher in my programming ability.

> **Make the most of every minute. Use lunch hours and free time to work on your idea or product, even if working full-time. But be careful not to overstep; your full-time job is the first priority when at work.**

My Radio Shack rotation went on for a few weeks, until I stopped in at an Apple Computer Reseller Store. I was able to play with an Apple computer that had a color screen and a nice basic programming language. This was January 1982, just one month after touching my first computer. I again went out and purchased every book on Apple Basic programming I could find. I was now writing Apple Basic programs. I was hooked. The computer had everything I needed to carry out all the ideas going through my head.

As a teacher I did not have a lot of free cash, but I had to have a computer. So I sold my new car and bought a used car, taking the difference to purchase an Apple computer, an extra floppy disk drive, and an Epson printer. (The total was over $3,000.) I thought I was in heaven. Everywhere I went I looked for more books. I was hungry for examples of programs others had written. Back then there was no Internet or Amazon to purchase books. There was no Google for looking up other programs. It was definitely the dark, unconnected age for self-taught programmers like myself.

Even though I was still teaching, programming became my life's passion. Every minute I was not teaching, I was jotting down lines of code. At first it was simply making a little box horse run across the screen. One of my friends who sold business software on minicomputers joked about my primitive, silly programs. He never thought I would make it in the computer field with an Apple — he thought of Apple computers as toys.

His criticism didn't discourage me. It just motivated me to push harder. I had ideas of what I wanted to do. I needed to learn how to make things move in a circle. Then move up and down. Everything was a new formula. My college education in math and physics seemed to come into play. I kept going to bookstores to find more books, with more examples. I needed to learn more so that I could make my animated simulations and follow this passion wherever it was leading me.

FOLLOW YOUR IMAGINATION

I knew that I had to create more sophisticated animations to make what I wanted to use in the classroom. By owning a computer, I was able to write code and type it into the computer and test right away. I could work all night without worrying about a store closing. My explanation to others about why I was so absorbed was that this was the first time in my life that I could take my imagination, put it in front of me, and then change what I came up with. This was good and bad: it meant every night programming into the wee hours. At school, I taught my classes, and every spare minute I was writing code or reading a book. And yet, it was so much fun, it was all I wanted to do. This was the passionate component of grit showing up again.

The first simulation I wanted to make was complex: it would show the moon revolving around the earth as the earth revolved around the sun. This was a simulation I carried out every year in my classroom, by moving all the desks to the side of the room and making a big circle on the floor. This circle represented the path of the earth. Then, by using a string, I would attach the earth to the moon. I revolved the moon around the earth as it travelled around the sun.

This is what I wanted to represent on my Apple computer. I worked on the formulas. This is where I developed the philosophy that the hardest part of a program should be done first. Once the most difficult calculations are complete, the rest would flow. It took days to figure out how to make a circle and then move that circle around another circle, while creating a path of dots to show the path of the moon. The difficulty of the problem was tempered by my passion for the work. This is another hallmark of the entrepreneurial spirit.

When completed, I showed the program to my science classes. Everyone loved it. The kids understood it, and I felt it was successful. By now it was late February 1982. I read about a software convention in Boston in late May. I noticed some of the vendors sold educational software for the Apple. There were a few vendors that focused on science software.

FINDING A SOFTWARE PUBLISHER

My story on finding the best publisher for my software.

D-day was here. The trade show in Boston was going to start tomorrow (a Saturday). I decided to drive to the show on the Saturday morning. I was ready with a full disk of color simulations relating to the Solar System. I had taken advantage of the color graphics capabilities on the Apple. I left my house in New Jersey at 4 a.m. I knew it was a five-hour drive to Boston, and I wanted to get there early.

I was there when the show opened, eager to learn about educational software and validate my own ideas. I walked the floor and found two publishing companies that sold science software. I looked at some of the software available and knew my stuff was equal if not better. I spoke with both publishers and was told to stop by at the end of the day when there were no more customers so they could look at what I had. I understood that they were here to sell and probably a lot of people wanted to show them stuff, most being a waste of their time.

Initially, I was upset that they would not listen to me right away. But I waited until the end of the day. I looked at every software vendor and read my books while jotting notes for new programs. About 30 minutes before the end of the day, one of the companies had an empty booth. I stopped by and showed my simulations. I was told that this was great, and I made an appointment to see them back in New Jersey.

I left that booth and went to the other publisher. Now it was five minutes before the end of the show. The vice president agreed to look at my disk. It was good enough that he stayed an extra 45 minutes and said this was some of the best science simulations he had seen. He also invited me to publish with his company in New York.

The trip to Boston was worth it. I was taking a chance on something I was passionate about, and I met with success.

This encouragement was all I needed. I left Boston around 6 p.m. and drove straight back to New Jersey, where I stayed up all night programming more simulations and making some changes that were recommended by the publishers. I could sense that my passion was turning into an opportunity.

MAKING BUSINESS DECISIONS

The publisher in New Jersey convinced me that his company would be a good match for my work. They promised to get my disks published quickly. They were supposed to review the entire set of programs and come up with comments and then lay out a schedule for getting it out the door and to customers. I agreed to a contract that had a 90-day clause, which would allow me to back out if I was not happy (it is always important to be careful with contracts).

KNOWING WHEN TO CUT BAIT

I wasted the next three months traveling back and forth, having meeting after meeting about the publication of my work even though the company was not making enough progress. This was a classic example of being sold on what the company could do in theory, rather than what could get finished. I had to make a business decision about whether to stick with this publisher — whose competence I had come to doubt — or work with the company in New York, which was well-established and more conservative.

I ended up taking my software to the publisher in Long Island, New York, in July of 1982. This company was successful and had a number of disks for social studies and math, with just a few science disks. My disks would really help fill out their offerings. They would help in writing the documentation wanted by schools (they had some excellent writers). I would need to keep writing software.

> **This publishing company taught me how important it is to make a product the best it can be before release. This mindset stuck with me forever.**

The company also did extensive testing on the software. At the time, it seemed to me that they were very picky about everything. But I came to understand what I saw as "picky" was a search for quality. I learned a lot about quality control from this group. It was hard for me to wait for them to test and get back to me with documentation changes. But they were right about making sure it was perfect, because they were selling on a national level and if things were not correct, it could hurt their reputation.

On my disks relating to the solar system, heart, earthquakes, and many others, the company hired college professors to confirm that all the simulations were accurate. The two initial disks were a great success (Solar System Simulator and Heart Simulator). The next disk was an earthquake simulation disk. The disk used animations to show different types of earthquakes and how the earth moved. The disk on earthquakes was not initially popular when released, until about six months later, when there was a significant earthquake in California. All of a sudden, my earthquake simulation was a best seller for the company for the next six months. Both the Earth/Moon disk and the earthquake disk won national awards for educational software.

The educational software portion of my life continued to generate additional income as a side venture. Educational software never became a full-time job; it was always there to subsidize my income while furthering my professional career. After these early successes, I developed for another four years and received royalties for 11 years. After the first four or five disks, I hired a student of mine to help with some of the programming since I was involved in other business activities. This student eventually went to college and when he graduated came to work for me full time as a programmer of business applications, in a business described later in this book. Educational software development was not a job that could support me full time, but it offered valuable experience and financial support as I began exploring other business opportunities.

> It is important to choose your business partners carefully. Make sure contracts have a way out in case things are not working out. Do the research before making the final decision. Make sure not to be sold on talk alone.

WHEN IS IT TIME TO LEAVE YOUR COMFORTABLE, SECURE JOB?

By June 1982, the local Apple store offered me a job to teach programming during a summer program to customers. The customers at the computer store loved my programming class, so in July of 1982, the store offered me a full-time job teaching and installing Apple computers and networks at schools.

> **Always confirm whether any outside work, ideas, or development are a conflict of interest for your full-time job. Some companies have a clause in their employment contract that describes how everything developed while working full time belongs to the company. Often, there is no problem if the ideas and products do not compete with or take any time from your full-time job.**

Leaving teaching was a tough decision. I would be taking a pay cut to leave 13 years of middle school teaching. But I would have a chance to learn a lot while continuing to write software to be sold nationwide to schools. The Apple store said there was no conflict of interest relating to me writing software to be published. The decision was difficult, but I chose to quit teaching at public schools.

Working for this Apple Reseller was going to give me the opportunity to learn all aspects of networking. I started by installing Corvus networks. This was connecting Apple computers to hard drives and printers via a Corvus network. The connection was via coax cables, and most networks for schools were within the classroom.

For me, the new job meant that I was driving to work on-site at the schools. I was part of a team for the first time. My position was on the technical side, handling installation, training, and supporting the sales team. What an education. I was learning everything from the ground up in real-time. I was working with professionals who were good at their business — it turned out to be very different from teaching. The day wasn't done when the bell rang. It was done when the network was installed correctly, even if that took until four in the morning. Like the other challenges I'd faced, this was very stimulating for me.

I was working with top administrators at schools and training teachers on the use of computers, including how to program in Basic on the Apple. There was also a language called Logo, which was based on geometric designs to teach math and programming. This was an excellent tool and still exists today in 2018.

> **Was it worth leaving the secure job? For me the answer was YES. This was more work, so much to learn, and so much fun. Sometimes in life you must follow your gut, take the leap and enjoy the ride.**

While working for the Apple Reseller, I had the opportunity to work with robots. One robot looked very similar to the original R2D2 from Star Wars. I had one that I could program to roll, talk, and move its arms. This was a lot of fun to program and demo. The robot was programmed with a simple language so children could learn to make it work. I worked with a robotic arm of the type that you see in a lot of films of industrial plants. I even wrote a program that had the arm type commands into an Apple computer that would change what the rolling robot would do. All this was a ton of fun and a great learning experience for me, and the students and teachers working with me.

Chapter 3:
From Education to Business

My move away from education was already underway, but at the Apple Reseller I was still ingrained in the education community. The real shift from education to business came when IBM launched the 8086 PC.

The new computer caught my eye, and I interviewed with a professional company in Secaucus, New Jersey, that worked with IBM PCs. It was made up of ex-IBM executives who broke off and started their own hardware/software company. They sold IBM minicomputers and their own custom payroll software.

When the PC came out, the new company could see that it was going to open a whole new world. Everything about the PC was fast, and they needed to hire programmers who could port old software and create new programs to take advantage of this new computer's power. I was first interviewed by a few individuals and then brought into a boardroom with eight others, sitting across from me at a large conference table. By the end of the interview I was offered a job. I accepted the position and gave notice at the Apple store, completing my transition away from education.

The company had specialized in software for the minicomputer and they were planning to open a division to focus on PC business applications. Small applications could be developed much more quickly on the PC, which made it a valuable business tool.

Working for a business company was a new experience. The company broke me in quickly. My first assignment was to go to Atlantic City to work on some computer applications at one of the large casinos. They wanted to get data into spreadsheets and a database on a PC-style computer.

After this initial break-in period for me, the company found a niche that I could handle on my own. During the early '80s, the fashion industry was looking for a quick and easily modifiable way to handle the tracking of clothes manufacturing in the areas around China, Vietnam, Japan, and other countries. The quantity and timing were critical to get orders to customers on time.

Back then, from the time a design was completed and the first threads, buttons, and lace were ordered, it was 18 months to final delivery. Materials shipped by boat, not airplane. One dress might start with material from Vietnam and lace from Japan, which would be shipped to China to be dyed, and then to Vietnam to be pieced. The entire process had to be ready on time for each specific season. My customers in New York were Yves St. Laurent, Calvin Klein, and Ralph Lauren.

Many long nights and holidays were spent in New York working side by side with the clients to develop software that would help these fashion houses manage the complete manufacturing cycle from the first order for material to receiving the finished product at the docks in the U.S. I developed a great relationship with these clients.

After working for the IBM-related business software company for eight months, I felt like I knew enough to go out on my own. I resigned from the position. It hadn't even been two years since I first met the Apple computer, and now I had five computers in my workroom. (Since there was no such thing as multi-tasking applications, I had to surround myself with multiple computers: one to program, another to test for bugs, and a third for taking notes and more.)

STARTING A NEW BUSINESS USING PREVIOUS CONTACTS:

This time I was not nervous about leaving a secure job to go out on my own. In order to build a new business, I used my contacts in NYC as well as working with some of the educational contacts I knew well from my days at the Apple reseller. The Board of Education in two townships hired me as a consultant. I continued to develop the educational software being sold by the Long Island publisher.

Over the next two years, I had consulting contracts with New Jersey school districts to plan teaching computer skills in first through twelfth grade. I trained the teachers in programming and business applications. I recommended Apple in the elementary (because of the educational applications available) and IBM for the high school (because of the business applications). It was my prediction that the IBM machines would be the most popular for business and that they should be used in high school for teaching typing, word processing, spreadsheets, and assorted other applications.

This consulting was very rewarding and profitable. Along with my education customers, I continued consulting and programming for the sales teams of Ralph Lauren, Calvin Klein, and Yves St. Laurent in New York, modifying the applications I had developed. (These New York customers had decided to follow me rather than stick with the company I had just left.)

In the early '80s, there were many employment contracts written when the personal computer was first released. Many people in the computer industry never thought the PC would amount to anything in the business market. Because of that, non-compete contracts were not always written

> **Make sure any contract you write for a new employee or partner includes non-compete clauses. This is important for protecting any intellectual property that might be developed at your company.**

or executed. In the age of consultants and outsourcing companies (by the late 1990s), non-compete contracts became a normal occurrence. Even customers sign contracts for not being able to hire employees from a consulting firm.

I continued to develop animated simulation software for the Apple to be sold through the publisher. My applications won awards, and in total I had developed 13 disks for Apple, handling educational simulations for many of the sciences.

I received numerous contracts relating to data mining, control systems for Law Firms, NASA, and a few from larger corporations. Most of these projects were one of a kind. I was learning and having fun but had a few reservations.

This was all great; I learned something new from every consulting job, and I wanted every challenge. The only drawback I found was that I was reinventing the wheel every time I worked on something new. I needed to find something I could do where I could capitalize on doing work once and use or sell it repeatedly. I still had a very limited budget, basically what I had saved over the last few years, but I was a determined entrepreneur.

STARTING A PRODUCT-BASED SALES & CONSULTING BUSINESS

After some research, I found a new opportunity. Small business owners needed a computer system and software to run their companies. Many of them had been using older minicomputers to run their businesses or worked a completely manual system.

By this point, minicomputers and their consultants were too expensive for small business owners. Just the upkeep of a computer system could end up being a large percentage of their yearly expenses. Could I provide a solution that was affordable? If I could solve that problem, I thought, I could create a scalable business around it.

But what software would I use to help small businesses reduce their computer and software costs?

I was not sure how to handle this problem. I had no knowledge of accounting / inventory systems. I knew next to nothing about business, except the little I had learned from my customers. I set out to find a solution. I went to the trusted bookstore and purchased books. I purchased magazines about personal computers.

Eventually, I ran across a tiny ad from a one-person company in Virginia. The owner had written an accounting system in dBase (a relational database) and had been selling it for a year. I was able to work out a deal with him where, with a one-time license fee, I could sell and modify the software for 99 years. (The only restriction was that I could not resell it to another developer without it being a specific solution-based sale.) I would be responsible for all maintenance of the software.

> **Whenever possible do not reinvent the wheel. If you can use something already created within your solution and the cost is either free or reasonable take that path as long as it saves you time (which means**

This software helped me to jumpstart a business idea, turning it into a reality. For a small amount of money, I was able to follow a dream, today, rather than a few years from now (or possibly never).

Now I had a way to learn, in real time, how an accounting system worked. I purchased a few books on accounting and was able to quickly pick up inventory, accounts receivable, and payables. The general ledger system took the most time to learn. I found out over time that many people never truly understand general ledger, which is why there are accountants in the first place!

Ultimately, as I worked to position my product and myself, I realized that general ledger wasn't as important to owners dealing with day-to-day operations as it was to accountants. More importantly, software products that focused on general ledger were weak in the other areas of business accounting that I already understood well. I could focus on the strengths of my own knowledge, and that would give me a competitive edge.

Through research into the topic of small business accounting and competitive products, I had defined my offering. By this point, I took the initiative of creating my own company: Mini-Byte Software. The name Mini-Byte Software came from the idea that it was a software company and the computers back then had very little memory (bytes) in the systems. Hence, Mini-Byte Software was created.

Now all I needed to do was figure out how to sell the software and hardware to go along with it. I first started talking to local businesses about how they managed their inventory and sales, including what they might need to improve their business.

The first business I found that needed my help was a lumberyard. Its major source of pain was not having good control of inventory and accounts receivable. It also needed to reduce the high cost of the mini-computer system to run its old software. Some products were purchased by weight, others by yards, bundles, gallons, or other methods of measure. Very few software products were flexible enough to handle all these physical traits, and software systems that were complex enough tended to be exorbitantly expensive.

> **To be successful in any type of business, it is important to listen to the customer and learn before going into all the details about your product or solution. Talk with the potential client, not at them. They know what they need and why they are looking.**

Most of the customers for my software had clients who were either small builders or homeowners who did not always pay bills on time, so handling the paperwork for accounts receivable was a major task. To sell my product, I demonstrated the inventory, invoicing, accounts receivable and accounts payable portion of my software.

I then explained another feature of the software that directly addressed one of the company's pain points: the inventory and how we could help control ordering so that the vendor's orders could match customer sales. This matching was a difficult task by hand. The company needed to be able to order products that would fill customer orders for anything not already in stock. If 6 foot, 2x4 lumber was needed, the company had to make sure to order enough to cover all open orders, plus some for inventory. Imagine tracking every order from each local builder and homeowner who needed 30 or 40 sizes of boards, and then consolidating them to make sure enough stock was ordered to fill those orders. Then when the stock was delivered to the lumberyard, the system needed to alert someone to pick the quantity needed for each previous order and set it aside for pickup or delivery. Prior to using a computer solution, this matching of inventory to customer orders was done by hand.

This is just one example of what the business software needed to be able to manage. Many companies used a combination of electronic tracking and manual matching to accomplish this task. My product would reduce the need for someone to always manually go through all customer orders when placing their orders to vendors. Then management was needed when receiving and then shipping paperwork to and from the correct vendor. Previously, available solutions ran on minicomputers costing tens of thousands of dollars with very high support and repair costs. That technology could easily put a company in financial debt. On the other hand, good technology could increase speed, accuracy, and customer satisfaction, while reducing the need for extra people in the back office.

Like many customers, this lumberyard needed modifications to what I considered my basic software product. They needed solutions for handling the point of sale. I developed a point of sale module that would communicate with inventory and accounts receivable, having the ability to print from any terminal printer. The complete solution needed many parts, all of which needed to be included in the proposal and then sale. The quote needed to include the cost for modifications of software, a server to run the application, terminals, keyboards, cash drawers, printers, cabling to each terminal located around the store and yard, etc. I needed to consider everything including small details like the metal ends to coax cables that plug into computers, a hub to attach all the remote terminals, and so much more.

> **This sales/customization approach is referred to as Resolving the Point of Most Pain. You do this, and you get the sale. And I did.**

Small businesses needed a solution that was affordable. In the mid-1980s desktop computers were expensive. Making a huge profit on hardware proved difficult at times. If I could offer a lower cost solution using a server and dumb terminals, I could keep the total hardware cost down while increasing software and consulting dollars. All of this while still being a total lower cost than competitors offering computer desktop solutions. In other words: the hardware problem was solved.

Most importantly, I learned that what I needed to do to make this sale was to provide solutions for the owner. The accountant wanted solutions for the general ledger, but the accountant was not the decision-maker. I was able to sell the software by solving the owner's point of sale and inventory needs, which worked real-time with the customized inventory modules.

> **What I learned from this experience, is that you need to convince the decision-maker, not necessarily the accountant.**

LESSONS LEARNED FROM TRYING TO CLOSE DEALS:

The lessons that I learned from this first foray into sales deserve some focus because they are useful principles for many businesses.

For smaller companies, make sure you are speaking with a decision-maker. Find out why they want a new solution for running their company. It might be to upgrade to faster computers, trying to save money on hardware costs and support, or because their current solution does not have the functionality needed for a changing business environment. Knowing which answer motivates their interest will help you frame your demo appropriately.

When relating to functionality, ask many questions about priorities and differences from the current solution that are needed for the decision-maker to be happy. Speak to others in the organization who need features the current system does not provide. All of these questions should be asked before giving the first demo of your software. By doing this you will be ready to present a solution that addresses their specific needs in the first meeting, when you have their best level of attention.

> **Selling is an art, and communication is your tool. Listen to the customers first, then ask questions to find out what they think they need. Being too aggressive might cause push-back and the possibility of losing a potential sale. Take your time and close the sale when the customer starts nodding "yes" and agreeing with you. You want to work with the customer to have them say," this is what I need."**

You might think that this is wasting a lot of time. What happens if they don't purchase your solution? I could be calling other potential customers with this time! Of course, that's true.

Find a company that absolutely needs something. Then make sure you can deliver a solution for that customer. An interested company with a need is a valuable commodity. If you have time and money invested in a solution that has a value, then you need to sell it because you believe in it. It is worth investing the time to make sure you have the best possible chance of closing the sale to this new customer on the first or second visit. (That doesn't mean getting the order, just getting the key person to say, "this is what I am looking for, now let's move forward.")

> **You can lessen the risk of wasting your time by correctly identifying companies that are worth making a sales pitch to.**

First impressions stick in a customer's mind. Remember that. It is very important that you do your fact-finding to make the first full sales presentation the best you possibly can. Do not try a first demo until you know what the customer wants or needs. Potential customers will be impressed and excited to find a professional willing to listen before trying to sell a solution. Forget computers for a moment: building a home has the same sales process. You want a builder who listens to what you want in the house, not what they want. Again, if you are selling a toaster, you will not spend a lot of time preparing for a demo, but you still need to ask questions, like how many pieces do you want to toast at one time, do you heat up bagels, etc. Listening goes a long way toward making your product a better fit and improving the impression you make on your potential customers.

CONSIDER WHAT IT WILL TAKE TO IMPLEMENT THE OVERALL SOLUTION — DOWN TO EVERY LAST DETAIL

For example, with a product like mine, I needed to consider going to the customer site and installing cables enabling communications from the terminals to the printers and the terminals to the server. Before delivery, software modifications needed to be completed and tested. Putting a price on systems, software, modifications, and installation can be disastrous for a technology company, if quoted incorrectly. It could be priced too high, putting you out of the market, or too low, where you might lose money. If you did not consider how any modifications might affect the rest of the solution, it could cause major issues.

When dealing with small business owners it is important to figure out who is responsible for running the company. Before ever trying to sell to that customer, you need to find out why they are looking for a new

> **Understanding your competitive landscape is a must for any company. You need to understand the alternative solutions your customer may use, or the alternative of "doing nothing" and sticking with their current arrangements.**

solution or system. Customers want to talk and tell you what they want. You have to find out what they need. They work with whatever they have every day and talk about it every night. This is their life, and if you can make it work better and solve their point of pain, they are going to become your champions and help you get the sale. So, talk to the customers before doing a demo; find out what they need. If they needed something that my software did not do and I could add a small feature by spending an hour or two writing some code, I would do it. For me, this small sacrifice gave me a better than 95% close rate for every demo I did. A few hours of

> **What really matters in a sale, is not the total price of the sale, but the profit. If the total price is lower but the profit is higher, everyone is happy.**

preparation to sell a base software package for $4,000 – $5,000 ($12,000–$15,000 in today's world) was worth it, especially with such a high close rate. I went after the pain points that were described to me by decision-makers and other important users. Once they would see their problems resolved on a screen, the sale would close. I couldn't understand why more companies wouldn't invest in that preparation time, but I was happy they didn't, or I might have not closed as many sales.

For my company, the differentiators were technical and cost-based. Most companies were either selling minicomputers with terminals or Microsoft and then Novell networks using PCs on each desk. I decided to use a multi-user system with inexpensive dumb terminals on each desk. This lowered the overall hardware cost. I was looking to keep prices down, efficiency up, and profit maximized.

A small business owner looks at the total price and if the solution works for them. The solution is based around the software. If their budget was $20,000 and the hardware cost me $11,000, then the remainder was the software. Since I owned the software, this was my highest profit area. If someone was offering the Microsoft or Novell solution, their hardware cost might have been $20,000 before software. As long as my solution did what was needed, the decision was easy. I won many deals by offering an equivalent or better solution for less money because of the network and operating system chosen. The total package is what counts. This same philosophy goes for many businesses selling products and services.

New customers such as a truck repair center and a number of other small companies needed similar systems for managing inventory, sales, and more. By this point, I felt confident in my product and decided I could hire a few employees full time. I hired a recent college graduate who wanted to learn how to program on PCs. He had learned how to program in a different language and had potential. Being a programmer myself and now an employer could have led to many new issues. How was I now going to relate to the other programmers, handle project management, and manage quality control? It was difficult to delegate tasks that I used to handle. However, the expanded team did give me the opportunity to find new customers and make more modifications.

BUILDING A BUSINESS AROUND MANUFACTURER LEAD REFERRALS

I was now able to sell my software system as a product, for a base price (with no cost and no time to program). Then I would add on the value of the modifications to create special versions. Once these special versions were created, I could sell into new vertical markets. (A vertical is a specific business area, such as retail, warehousing, medical, manufacturing, etc.) Then services were added for additional income.

The company that developed and sold Xenix was SCO (Santa Cruz Operation). I spoke with SCO when purchasing operating systems to include with my sales. Because Xenix systems were not a "run of the mill" solutions in the mid-1980s, I was building a reputation of being able to sell this specialty product and related solutions to small business owners in the tri-state area of New Jersey, New York, and Pennsylvania.

By developing this relationship, I was able to start receiving leads. SCO had internal sales people who made money when operating systems shipped to resellers or customers in their territory. They ran ads to attract customers. The customers would want to purchase the operating system if they had a solution to run on it. Because of this, SCO set up a VAR (Value Added Reseller) channel. The VAR had the solution that ran on the operating system. This was the added value, hence the name VAR.

Because I was a small, unknown company, I wanted to get leads from SCO. If SCO recommended my company, it was giving me a stamp of approval, so there was some initial trust from the customer. I quickly learned how to get the SCO sales staff on my team. The first thing I did was to close every deal they sent my way. I would do whatever it took to close the deal. I would discount if there was another dealer trying to sell the same thing. If they had an application need, I was the only one in my company the customer spoke with. With this personal touch, I was lucky to have an advantage over larger companies. A larger company would have sales people who were not programmers, system designers, or very familiar with the software solution. So, when I was competing against other companies, I had a combination of sales expertise with knowledge of all the technical ins and outs of the solution needed by the customer. As a result, an SCO sales person would rather send a lead to someone with a high close rate (like myself).

Then there were other things I would do to make an SCO sales person happy. At the end of every quarter, a sales team needed to make a quota, so they wanted to sell extra operating systems. Because I had a successful business and knew I was staying in the business, I would purchase extra stock of operating systems to sell for the next month. Most other VARs purchased as needed, not for inventory. The sales people at SCO loved that I did that. This is the same for almost any business. If I sold other products, the manufacturer would have the same goals, and if I looked for leads, I would buy extra inventory if it meant being higher on the list to get leads.

When a business owner would call SCO about using the Xenix operating system to run their systems in New Jersey, I would usually get the lead, and that was because of good customer feedback.

> **To get leads, you must build a good relationship with the reps at the manufacturer. Find out what you need to do, to get high on their list for leads.**

A FULFILLMENT CENTER, SIMILAR TO EBAY AND AMAZON, JUST SMALLER

My next potential customer was a fulfillment center, which means a warehouse, order fulfiller, and shipper for other businesses. It would warehouse products for its customers and ship when orders were placed. When a business got an order for products, it would fax it to my new customer (the fulfillment warehouse). The owner would then pick the items, pack them, and ship for the original business customer. This is very similar to Amazon today.

This fulfillment business had a handful of customers, and the owner wanted to grow his client base. The business was complicated because he would get inventory deliveries for all of his customers. He had to manage and separate inventory for each of these business customers. He needed an accounting system to manage inventory for all his customers and reliably produce invoices and shipping tickets for all of their customers. Then he needed to charge his customers for housing their inventory, billing, and shipping orders. My customer wanted to grow his business, but everything was getting too confusing because he was not able to track multiple companies at the same location.

This was going to be my largest programming job yet. Currently the warehouse used several individual computers (one for each of its clients) and spent a large portion of its profits on programming and maintenance of the systems. There was a lot of work to do. First, I had to come up with the quote for programming and the hardware system so as not to lose money. This was a task that could not be taken lightly. This is one of the many difficult parts of running a company and modifying software. Back in the late 1980s, the tools currently available did not exist. A lot of estimating was seat of the pants, using a spreadsheet or on paper — meaning it was risky and not accurate. I gave my customer a very detailed quote for the software and systems.

> **Quoting effectively and efficiently is a crucial part of the sales process and the company growth process. Every quote for product modifications must be very detailed. If something is too general and could be interpreted differently, it could cost you hundreds of hours of programming time.**

Put everything in writing; go over it with the customer (even though many do not have the time and don't think they need to go over all the details). Many software companies go out of business because they do not take the time. It is needed anyway so that your programmers understand exactly what they need to do. Anytime you modify or create a software product, new ideas always come up and jobs grow (called scope creep). As a business owner, you need to be savvy to identify scope creep and you (or your team members) need to raise a flag when it begins to happen, so that you can push back against customer requests and point out that the cost will go up.

Many companies skimp on the preparation of quotes. These companies quite frequently end up hiring lawyers to resolve issues with customers losing time and money on lawsuits. My advice is to make sure complex quotes are checked over more than once prior to delivery. Whether it is building a house, creating a new wedding dress, setting up an office, catering an event, quoting a new network, designing a software solution, or designing a new generator, the planning phase is crucial and too often skimped on.

Let someone else look over the wording of what is included and what you are responsible for within the specifications. Many times, customers will go back to a quote or email, point to a specific paragraph and say, "but you said this." These are some of the many things that can cause issues later. Take that extra few minutes, read over that proposal, letter, or email to make sure it is grammatically correct and does not promise or imply things you do not mean to offer. Make sure that your quotes and letters are not vague enough to be interpreted in any alternative way. I say this with experience. In all the years of having businesses, I never hired a lawyer for any customer issues.

The warehouse customer accepted my estimate, which included what I understood he needed. The job was accepted, partially because he could not find anyone else to do it within his budget. Why was I willing to do it cheaper than everyone else? Easy: I was going to sell the complete solution, over and over again, once I'd learned all about warehousing from my new customer.

Every time I got involved with a new customer business, I thought of it as a learning experience, and the value of the specific job also included the knowledge and future business that it could bring.

> **According to Forbes, 9 out of 10 startups fail, which is why friends and family might be nervous for you.**

This job took about a month to complete. All the while I was selling other systems, creating quotes, and running my company, now with two full-time employees and one part time. I worked every day from 7:00 a.m. to 11:30 p.m. If I was making a lot of progress, I would stay even later. This was basically my schedule every day, including weekends. I would try to take off Saturday night. But this business was a personal challenge. It was my life, my passion—and I had the grit to commit to an intense schedule. Everyone who knew me thought that I picked a very difficult road considering the number of people who fail when starting a business.

But I knew I could do it. I got the job done. SCO was getting calls from my customers complimenting us on a good job. And because of this, I was getting more leads than any company in New Jersey. For difficult software solutions, I was getting leads from New York and Pennsylvania. It was amazing!

My business kept growing. Because of a reputation for closing deals and selling the Xenix operating system, I continued to get leads for small-business owners needing a solution to run their operations. The leads came from all over the tri-state area. I needed to increase the capabilities of the company so that we could build the computers and the systems to fulfill the needs of these new customers.

By this point Mini-Byte had about 10 employees, but that was not big enough for potential large customers to trust that I would be around in five years. During the 1980s and 1990s many companies (startups) came and went. Many of their customers got burnt, paying money for jobs that were never completed or systems that could not be supported. Therefore, I had to go above and beyond to prove my company was viable.

The first thing I did was get an impressive office space. I set up a large lab for building computers and a room for training, even though we didn't do much training. Secondly, I made sure customers received excellent support, even when that challenged our small staff. It was difficult to find the help that was both technically reliable and good with people. When interviewing programmers I would ask them to write small applications that needed to be completed and running within a couple of hours while they were at my office. If they could not do this, they were not technically qualified for my company. If it was someone for support, they either needed to know about computers and networking or about accounting systems for running a business, and they had to have excellent people skills.

> **Hiring the right employees can be very difficult. Sometimes, I would start with individual interviews then a team interview. I asked potential employees to write a small application that tested their knowledge. Some people can talk the talk, but not walk the walk.**

During the 1997–2001 time frame, there weren't enough consultants to handle the strong internet growth and the Y2K issue. I knew of one consultant who was great at interviewing, would get hired at $250/hr. It would take the employers about two months to figure out he was not knowledgeable and then fire him. Make sure to always check references before hiring a consultant.

At this point, I was learning an incredible amount about what it took to run a business. After initially learning about technology, I was now switching to learning about entrepreneurship and business operations. This was, of course, another challenge that I dove into with passion and determination. Here are just a few of the important findings that became clear to me during this period.

EVERY LEAD NEEDS A RAPID, ACCURATE FOLLOW-UP

When I received a lead, I needed to be the first company to give a complete quote. I usually quoted fixed pricing even for programming. This gave me a great advantage over other companies. I was able to figure out about how long it would take me to write the program or the modification. The quote was based on that number. My programmers would work on the quoted specifications during the day. If they got stuck, I would fix it at night when they left. (It's important to remember that as the owner, it is your responsibility to make sure the job is completed on time and the customer is happy.) The same would happen with setting up computers with a multiuser operating system. At night I would work on resolving any issues. During the day I was busy selling, visiting clients, and making sure the right products were ordered. Luckily I was still young, in good shape with lots of energy. If I spoke with a potential customer about a system and software at 4 p.m., I would work on the quote and send it out by midnight so that it would be on their fax in the morning (yes, back then faxing was the standard, not email). Many customers told me that if they could get that kind of attention before a sale was made, they knew they had found the right company. I have known some companies that think if you send a quote too quickly, the potential customer will think you are too anxious to get the sale. But guess what: that quick response is exactly what the customer wants.

TAKING A CHANCE, CREATING A PROTOTYPE:

I can remember going into a slightly larger company that did a lot of work for the government. It needed to track every job — every document, letter, and specification. It also needed to group them for easy access for any complicated government job. I went in and described a solution where a scanner capable of scanning 50 pages at a time could be used to scan in documents and then store them in a database. The meeting was on a Wednesday and went well. They knew that any system like that would cost over six figures. I was proposing that I could deliver a system for a fraction of that cost. I knew the only way to get the deal was to show a prototype as quickly as possible.

I went back to the office and found the right Fujitsu scanner to handle the scanning task. I ordered it next day delivery so that I could have the equipment to test out the software I was going to write over the weekend. I would scan documents with links to a database that controlled what project they belonged to, as well as keywords, dates, etc. I had a feeling that if I could show the company a working model, they would order it. I never doubted myself as far as figuring out how to do it, or even whether I could get it done based on my self-imposed schedule. I knew that if a larger customer such as this would buy my solution, I could sell it over and over again to this new vertical market.

I worked the entire weekend on this prototype. By Monday morning, I had developed a working model for handling and saving documents in a database, organizing them by job, and giving the user a way to pull them up on the screen. The solution was not complete, but it worked well enough for a demonstration. I called the potential customer Monday morning to set up an appointment for that week. I took the equipment to the customer, showed a demo with their documents, and closed the deal. At this time, I gave the project to one of my programmers to finish the user interface, the printing piece, and other parts that were not yet functional. I did the debugging of the software after the programmer thought it was complete. Again, I went with my programming model: develop the hardest part first, and when that's working you can make it pretty. This was hard work, but creating something new was also so much fun.

> **This again illustrates a unique aspect of successful entrepreneurs – they sense which directions will yield growth and which ones won't.**

Once the solution was running, I was able to sell it to a number of other companies. I did not make a lot of money on the first sale, but it was an investment in creating a product that could be duplicated. What was unusual about this specific case was that I had to order new equipment and then write software all on a gut feeling that if I had a working prototype, I just knew I could close the deal. It was another example of grit and a vivid demonstration of the power of a working prototype.

Working with a warehouse/distribution client to develop a new solution to pick orders more efficiently

Another example of the prototype as a sales tool related to a warehousing solution. I visited a potential customer, H-Imports, with an import and manufacturing business that was growing quickly. The person in charge of IT and running the warehouse was sharp and ambitious, and he recognized that new computers could provide much better solutions to solve his problems. Currently nothing was available for the PC market, only the mini and mainframe. The price of those systems, software, and maintenance was out of the range of his company and others its size.

I spent a few days with him, learning all about his inventory and how the orders were picked and then shipped. He needed to track when an item was received, who or what order it was for, whether it was needed for manufacturing or just for shipping, what product it related to, and what customers were involved. Many orders had multiple line items. They had a large warehouse—60 feet high with five or six levels of inventory — and picking could occur from anywhere in the building. Forklifts were key for picking orders, but they could not easily pass in the thin aisles, meaning that pickers regularly got in each other's way. It was taking at least twice as long as it should to pick orders. Something needed to be done to eliminate the aisle bottlenecks without rearranging the entire physical warehouse layout. How could the picking be more efficient without spending a few years of profit trying to get it working on a minicomputer?

> **Successful entrepreneurs must think outside the box and come up with new ideas to handle current problems.**

I worked on this solution prior to my next visit. Before going back to see H-Imports, I thought about how to program a way to have a picker go out and pick similar items for multiple orders in one trip (currently a picker would pick one order at a time). Then the shipping person could sort the picked items into the specific orders, but the picker would have saved time moving around the warehouse. This alone was going to resolve their first major issue. So the question was: how could software help with this problem. The first idea I came up with was to batch orders and separate them for picking. In other words, one person would not pick an entire order; he would only pick the items in his assigned aisles. The computer could handle this, though it would have been an impossible task for humans. Imagine going through a batch of orders and picking out the items in aisle 4 and giving that to one picker. Orders would be divided by what was in different aisles. So one picker goes down aisle 4 and picks items for 7 partial orders. Then they go down the next aisle and pick for those orders, and possibly two other orders. The same type of thing would be done by the other five pickers, in their assigned aisles. It was possible that a picker might go to aisle 12, the bin fourth from the end, and the third level high to pick 14 widgets, which might be found on five different orders. The picker only knew what was on his or her list, not what was in every order.

Then, the computer would also help the workers organize all of the picked items into specific orders. The warehouse had a receiving area. Products received would be sorted and put on shelves based on locations already in the computer. When orders were picked they would be brought to a shipping/sorting area for boxing and printing of shipping labels.

The same computer-generated list that told pickers where to get items would tell them where to drop the items off at the receiving area. So items picked would be dropped off on the floor (or table) where all sorters would drop separate items into areas for each order. The sorters had the job of matching the picked items to the orders getting prepared to ship. The pickers could then pick up their next sheets to pick the next set of orders. The sorters/packers would do the final separating of items for each order because they were already in the same physical location.

A successful prototype could morph into other completed products, in this case, a warehousing system:

When I came back, I met with my customer. My prototype was not completed, but I was able to demo five orders being divided into picking lists based on what was in each aisle, not by order. This could save the company money and cut down on the congestion in the warehouse aisles. The Operations Manager loved it, and H-Imports quickly became my customer. They not only purchased the software and modifications but also a new computer system (running Xenix), server, and service.

The problem of congestion in the aisles was gone. The time savings was dramatic. Overtime was cut, and deliveries were not often late. Everyone was happy and became spoiled. Within six months the customer came back and asked if we could make the system tell us how to be more efficient, again.

There was a way to do this. In the past items were put into the warehouse based on size and where they had been for years. With this computer system it was possible to know which were the items that sold in higher volumes. To make things more efficient, high volume items should be placed lower down, so the picker did not need to waste time going up to a higher level on the forklift. So the system would print reports that recommended the higher volume items to be placed on lower shelves. This again saved a lot of time, since going up and down from a higher bin was not fast.

Since the software had an excellent live customer willing to give testimonials, the time was right. I now started selling the warehouse software without the rest of the accounting application (unless needed). It had taken on a life of its own.

The warehouses interested in purchasing the software were bigger and bigger. One of the warehouse groups wanted to own the software, and they were interested in selling it themselves as part of a package of services to other warehouses. We worked out a deal where they purchased the software outright and I let them hire the main programmer/support person on the project. It was at the right time, since at that point my Unix integration system was growing.

TAKE RESPONSIBILITY:

A story about fixing issues as quickly as possible (always trying to save the client):

I was able to land a few large customers during this era, including Ericsson GE, Charles Schwab, AT&T, Mellon Bank, and others. As a small business owner, I had my hands in everything being done in

> It's crucial for owners to stay on top of any potentially important issues so they do not escalate out of control.

the business (sometimes considered micro-management). I was responsible for all employees, equipment sold, software, and service. If something went wrong, I took it as my responsibility to make sure it was resolved (I managed the interaction with the customer if there was a larger issue). I did not usually handle the execution of fixing the issue if it was hardware or software. If I handed-off finding a resolution to someone else and the employee did not handle it correctly, the owner (me!) would be the one in court or getting bad reviews. Never think that because your employees screwed up, they need to be the ones to fix it with your customer. Remember, they are the employees; you are the owner. Take responsibility for everything coming out of your business.

> **Every owner should know what is important to himself or herself. Do you want to grow the company to 50+ people or keep it small? If you grow it, does your profit increase or just the total sales? Which is more important to you, having more sales or more profit?**

The problem with micro-managing is that it is difficult to grow past a certain size. In my case, I was comfortable having an average of 9–12 employees. When I did grow to 18 employees, I could not oversee all aspects of the business and felt like I was losing control. I needed to be within my comfort zone. If you work within your comfort zone, you will be much happier as an entrepreneur.

LEARN TO MAKE THE BEST OF SOMETHING THAT GOES WRONG:

One story about cabling and networking took place in a large office building in New Jersey. I quoted a division of Ericsson GE for a job that included cabling a new office for networking computers and printers. Ethernet cabling needed to be installed to each location. To create a quote like this you must first consider the amount of cable and cable connectors needed. Then you need to calculate the time needed to fish the cables through the ceiling and down inside the walls, and then to install the cable plugs in the wall, etc. Many of these cabling jobs needed to be done at night since there were people in the office during the day. I put together the quote and won the job. Over the course of a few nights, my crew was able to complete the cabling and testing. Everything looked good.

The customer plugged in their computers. Everything looked fine. Over the course of a few weeks, we received some support calls relating to computers losing connection to the network. I sent one of the technicians to the customer and everything looked ok. After the fourth call, we decided to try running a direct cable from the server to the computer to see what would happen. This worked fine, but other computers were having the same problem. This was becoming an issue.

After a few trips to the customer site, we figured there must be interference affecting the cabling. I did research and made phone calls. There was a new type of cable available that was less susceptible to interference from things like fluorescent lights (which are in drop ceilings where cable is run). During this time, the customer set up a meeting with company executives, basically to listen for a solution or fire my company and ask for their money back.

Since we had done some business with them before and there was potential for more business, we needed to fix the problem and satisfy the customer.

> **The lesson here is to prepare, especially when you have an idea what the meeting is about. Dealing with a problem is like a sales presentation: don't go in without having a game plan. What are you willing to do or give up in order to make this customer happy?**

I had to make some important decisions. I knew what the meeting was about, and I needed to prepare. I made my decisions up front so that I could control the conversation, which I knew was important. If you let the customer control the meeting, it will probably not end up well. Even if you want to control and guide the conversation, you must also make sure you listen to the customer so that you understand what is wrong (they might not know what the solution is).

In a very few cases, you might plan on an exit strategy with the customer, just because they are difficult and take up way too much time and effort. Decisions like that should be made prior to any important pre-scheduled meeting.

I came to the meeting and was taken to a boardroom with 10 executives sitting opposite me. This could have been rather intimidating since I was alone, but remember, I was prepared. I was told they were going to bring another company in to rewire the office and expected not to have to pay for the job we did. I explained to them that the issue with the cabling had nothing to do with the job we did, and the interference was related to a defect in the cables. Now, here is where many small companies would make the mistake of trying to get the customer to pay for something. I asked for no money and offered to replace all the cables at no cost to them (at night so as not to interfere with people working). If it didn't work, I would give them a full refund for everything. They had me leave the boardroom for a few minutes and then agreed to let me change all the cables. The meeting went well because prior to the meeting I thought about all the possible scenarios and had solutions for all of them. It was more important for me to have a happy customer than to worry about $5,000 worth of cabling and labor (today

> **What I learned from this event is: don't try to make too many excuses, blame someone else or try to get the customer to pay for something they purchased that didn't work.**

that would be equivalent to $20,000 — not an insignificant amount, but worth it for an important customer).

My original champion at the company told me that it was one of the smoothest solutions he had ever heard and that if I really could fix the problem they had several other jobs he would pass to me. I ordered the new cabling. We went up and installed the cables (it was easier than the first time because we could attach new cables to the old ones by taping the two together then pulling them through the ceiling. We were also able to pull them through the walls without having to re-fish everything). The job went perfectly, everything worked, the customer was happy, and we received new orders that more than made up for the money and time I'd spent making them happy.

Just bite the bullet, fix whatever is wrong and make a happy customer. Never get into a heated discussion. Avoid bad feelings, and never mention suing or lawyers. Sometimes you need to let a customer vent, other times you can offer a solution immediately and then an entire meeting can go smoothly with a positive outcome. Remember that it costs a lot to get a new customer — keeping one you currently have is a much better solution as long as it is a good customer and not one that is unhappy or abusive to your employees.

Don't panic when business slows down; act strategically:
People handle situations in different ways. Attitude is very important to being successful in business. It is particularly important to react quickly to changing environments. If something is not working, think about it, be critical, and make changes sooner rather than later. At the same time, don't panic.

I can remember there were a few times of the year, every year, when business would slow down in the computer software/hardware world: usually December, July, and August. Then there were those days when we would get a snowstorm and the phones would not ring.

Early on I would pace the floor and think, "What should I do?" I never wanted even one month where there was not enough money to pay the bills and make a profit. Should I take a break, go on vacation, or sleep in late? Nope. Ultimately, I made summers

> **Make sure to always work on managing your pipeline of booked and projected work. It is important to keep employees productive and to have a constant source of revenue.**

some of the best business seasons of the year. I figured out that many of my competitors went on vacation, but most of their customers were still working, and I was available. To deal with the holiday slow-down I would call customers to remind them that, if they made a large profit that year, maybe they should spend more money in December on what they needed for their businesses to reduce their taxes in April. A lot of small-business owners don't have time to think of those things. Many accountants don't know how much profit a company is making until months later. But the person who owns and runs a small business usually has a gut feeling about whether they are making money and having a good year. Appealing to their knowledge and offering a solution was a way I was able to deal with slow periods.

One of the differences was that, as an owner, I was responsible for most of the sales of my small company. The inner tempo of the company relied on me. If the phone stopped ringing, I would go back through my notes of previous contacts and call them or send faxes. (During the 1980s and the first half of the 1990s, faxes were still the best form of online communication. Email was mostly used in large corporations and usually internally.) I called or faxed my vendors and asked if there were any leads, and I had to do this proactively before my employees ran out of work.

> **Many people exhibit burnout and for many it might be a good time to take a few days off and relax. Not all entrepreneurs need this time off, but it is important to monitor.**

During the slow periods, my outbound sales calls increased dramatically and our business usually went very well. I would remind my customers this was a good time to upgrade because upgrading is easier when business is slow. I would pay a visit to my customers where there was potential to upgrade. We would talk about his or her business, and I would keep asking questions to find something we could potentially change in the software to make the company more efficient.

So what can you take away from a slow period in your business? Regroup quickly, and then do something different. Instill more energy into the company. Do not sulk. Do not say, "woe is me." Do not figure it is someone else's fault. You are the one who can make a difference, and it can be made now.

LEARNING TO DEAL WITH IMMORAL EMPLOYEES

Of course, being in business isn't all about your product and your relationship with customers. It's also about your relationship with your own team members, especially those who report to you. I must tell you a story about how innocent I was in the 1980s and early 1990s. Part of the business I created was building PCs and servers. At that time, it was 386, then 486, then Pentium computers. All the pieces would come from different vendors. I had four technicians who handled building computers, installing networks, and general computer support, as well as an employee for shipping and receiving.

Sometimes we would be missing a motherboard or two and memory chips. Because we were doing enough volume, I assumed that possibly the parts were being thrown out with the garbage (motherboards came in pizza-type boxes and the chips were very small). More than a few times, I would go out to dig in the dumpsters looking for boxes that might still have motherboards in them. The last thing on my mind was that maybe I could not trust my employees. Well, I never found any motherboards in the garbage.

My office manager, who had worked in retail, told me that someone was stealing; I just could not believe it. Eventually, I had to face the fact that these parts were missing on purpose. Now I had to consider what else was missing. I needed to tighten up watching the inventory. The system I was selling to my customers already handled the tracking of what inventory I should have. I had to watch my employees when they left for lunch, for jobs, and at the end of the day. This was not something I was accustomed to doing, and it was wasting my time, which was needed to continue with sales and programming.

Within a few months, I had let two employees go — the two I had decided were responsible for the missing items. I did not call the police or press charges. I paid them and just walked them out the door. Did I make the right decision? Well, I did not lose any more inventory. Did it hurt for a while? Yes! I learned that I could not trust all employees to work for the best interest of the business. More importantly, I had to find replacement technicians and they had to learn what we did. The need to understand the Unix operating system, multi-processor systems, and networking made it more difficult to find replacements, and the training time was not short.

I found out later that the two employees went to work for a worldwide cosmetics company. They got good jobs because of the experience gained at Mini-Byte. I did not give them a bad reference, because I never actually caught them with products going out the door. Later I found out that they were fired for stealing over $150,000 in computer components from the cosmetics company. This company also did not press charges because it was not good for morale. This made me feel a little less like a fool and proved to me that letting the employees go was the right decision.

> **If you have a gut feeling that something is going wrong in your company, follow your instincts. Figure it out and fix the problem. Waiting can hurt your company and can affect your employees. Waiting can also drain time and effort from positive activities such as sales, customer support, and rewarding employees who are doing a good job.**

A STORY OF RISK AND SLEEPLESS NIGHTS FOR A LARGE CLIENT

Sometimes, big opportunities involve big risks, and big sacrifices, to make them successful. I landed an opportunity to potentially create an entire trading floor for a large Wall Street trading company in Jersey City. This trading company was building out a space in a new building to move some of its business out of New York. This was a big deal: I was going to supply all the software and all the hardware for the installation. I was able to convince the potential customer that my company had the resources to build a network for a new trading facility with over a hundred workstations/servers. I needed to provide a new version of the Unix operating system that was needed for the Sybase database to be used for this solution. It entailed replicating the servers so that there was no single point of failure.

The developer for the new application, which would replicate data for close to one hundred percent uptime, visited my location, and we instantly hit it off. This consultant became my champion to supply the solution for the trading company. He was taking a chance because my competitor Sun Microsystems was a much safer route.

Part of the decision might have been relating to budget. The Mini-Byte solution was quite a bit less money than Sun, and Sun would take some of the service time away from the consultant.

> **Think about it: not taking a risk is the only strategy that is guaranteed to fail.**

Therefore, going with my solution saved money on hardware, freeing up more for the software and the consulting portion of the entire installation. After many interviews and visits, I received the contract based on meetings, reputation, and the customer's belief that Mini-Byte Software could deliver. The deal was that if at any time they believed I could not deliver, they could cancel the contract and I would have no recourse. This was the only part that was scary, since I had to purchase all the parts to build the servers and workstations ahead of time.

Since this was the largest deal I had ever done, my vendors would not supply all the equipment needed without a line of credit, which meant collateral. I was nervous about the opportunity because Intel, SCO, and Sybase had never tested their software on this newest board by Intel (so there might be issues). I had quite a bit of cash in the bank, but I needed more, so I put up my house as collateral for a short-term bank loan. This is a large risk, and one that many entrepreneurs take at one point or another.

> **Risk is something that every successful entrepreneur has taken. You must extend past your comfort zone to get those extraordinary opportunities. This is part of what sets successful entrepreneurs from those who fail.**

During this project, there were two major issues that I had very little control over. The newest version of the operating system was not stable on Intel's newest chips. Because of this, the database was having issues (just as a reference, Sybase worked perfect on Sun Microsystem machines). I was on the phone with SCO every day. I realized that I was going to have to get SCO to move faster. Even though it was an Intel motherboard, I sent two complete machines FedEx next day to SCO so they could test on the machine that needed to work for the trading company. The trading company was also an important win for SCO, so this installation did get some extra attention — beating out Sun Microsystems for a financial institution was almost unheard of.

I coordinated between Intel and SCO to make sure everything was completed by the time building construction was done at the trading company. Luckily for me, the construction took longer than anticipated! The original due date for delivery was held up because the rooms were not physically ready. I played my cards and never let on that I was worried because the software/hardware combination did not work without crashing. (If I had let on, they would have switched to Sun Microsystems in a minute; the database was already running on those systems.) This was a major issue. Cancelling the order would hurt my company. Just to be clear, the software was running on the SCO platform, just not with the newest Intel chip set which was competing with Sun.

On a Thursday, I received a call from the trading company that the room was going to be ready on Monday. I was getting a new version of the OS on Friday. I spoke with the developer in charge for the trading company and convinced the project lead to only take 6 machines on the first day since there was no way they would be able to get more than that up and running in one day. I convinced them that we would deliver 15 machines per day after the first day until they were all installed.

I finally received a new version of the OS from SCO on Saturday morning. The hardware needed to be changed and the OS needed to be installed on every machine. Once installed, the OS needed to be tweaked to get it to run. I still did not let on to the customer that there was a problem. Remember, my house was on the line, and if this deal failed, we would be stuck with 120 machines. I worked all weekend through Saturday night until Sunday late morning. When I finally had six machines running, I slept a few hours, then woke up and finished the last four machines. The next morning, two of my employees delivered the systems and each one worked. Over the next two weeks we delivered machines every day. The

> **Never bring up your personal or business issues to a customer. You are there to solve their problems. You should be friendly to customers, just don't try and make them your friend.**

server room was set up first, then a few weeks later, the trading room was complete, and the machines were ready for the traders. Forty-five days later, payment was received, and I was able to clear my debt. Prior to that I had never had any debt other than standard accounts payable invoices. The job was a risk, but it increased my company's reputation with SCO, which meant more leads.

What did I learn from this experience? Larger companies (like SCO, Intel and Sybase) are not usually in the same rush mode as a small company fighting to make a deadline or keep a deal. Keeping your cool, never letting a minute go by without moving toward your goal, not expecting that someone will remember to call you back, and knowing that other companies have their own agendas and issues are essential for a small business owner. If someone indicates they need something, like a test computer, send it to them knowing they will remember that they owe you a favor for your help (without saying anything). You need to be aggressive without getting anyone annoyed. You need to make it personal without explaining any personal issues like having to put up collateral to get the money to complete the deal. You can talk about how the order might be lost if the deadline is not met. Just be careful, remember that whatever you say, you cannot take back mistaken words.

Always be careful when speaking, think without taking too much time, and remain calm, even in the face of stress and concern about the risks you've put on the line for the deal.

Chapter 4:
Deepening Expertise and Changing Technologies

In a technology business, it's important to strategically evaluate new technologies. (This is true in any business, though instead of technologies you may be evaluating trends, products, or fashions.) It's important to know when to go for the "next big thing" and when to say no.

When dealing with technology, magic means money. When a technology is new and not many people understand it, you can charge more money for consulting and for the product. If it seems "magical," it is worth more to consumers. As a product becomes a commodity and more people adopt, the competition drives down the price and profit. It's no longer magical. It was always my goal to stay at the edge of new technology, get the higher rates, and work the magic.

I said no to new technologies multiple times. In October 1990, I worked with Chorus Systems (a company based in France) on the possibility of bringing a distributed system technology to the Unix reseller channel in the U.S. This was a type of parallel processing using Intel Motherboards. It would mean getting into a new market, which was very exciting to me. But, even though it seemed exciting, I was not willing to give up what was already working to take this chance. After evaluating the technology, I decided it was not time for this to be successful in a business environment, but possibly it could be in research and educational markets. Because of this, I made recommendations to the company in France, but I did not pursue it further for my own business. The decision was based on working within my expertise, which was the business world.

In 1991, I decided the NeXT computer was the future. It had a Unix operating system and a great graphical interface. NeXT had been started by Steve Jobs before his second round with Apple. I was really excited about a graphical user interface for applications running on Unix. By jumping in early, I wanted to take advantage of working in a familiar environment with a company started by Steve Jobs. The only thing it needed was a database supporting the platform, and I could write code and sell it as a high-end workstation to the many customers I already had. I was able to invest in becoming an early adopter because I already had a successful Unix integration business. This was taking a chance to get involved with something at an early stage.

After a few months, I was starting to regret jumping in early. The databases did not come for the market I was involved with. Luckily, it did not take a lot of attention from my already well-running business. I spent time late at night working on the NeXT and waiting.

This investment was a failure due to a lack of NeXT applications and the price of the systems. There is a possibility Steve Jobs was negotiating with Apple at the time, which meant not focusing on applications or databases, but we will never know. Had more developers known this was actually the future of Apple, things might have been different. But NeXT got out of the hardware business two years later. The systems were technically as good as many of the Apples offered just a few years ago. It was great technology, but it was also a little too early for the business world.

Thankfully, my core business was strong while I took this risk, and I could recover. My only loss was the investment in the NeXT machines, which amounted to about $30,000 (in today's world that would be close to $60,000). I did eventually sell the systems I purchased at a loss, and it was another valuable lesson learned.

> Not all decisions are good ones, but successful entrepreneurs make sure they have a working business while they take risk and they don't "bet the farm" on any one gamble.

During the same time period, from 1989 to 1991, I was involved in selling early stage multiprocessor systems built to run Xenix and Unix operating systems. Because of the combination, small-business owners could get minicomputing power out of systems running multiple Intel 486/25 MHz chips on the same machine. I started selling systems made by Corollary, the premier multiprocessor hardware vendor of the time. It was a small company with smart people. I also sold Zenith multiprocessor systems (yes, Zenith made some powerful computers back then). Some of the systems being sold had proprietary chipsets and proprietary drivers. One multiprocessor system I decided not to sell was made by a small company in California. It had its own chips designed to run with SCO. During my testing, I found too many standard applications that did not work correctly for me to consider it reliable. I had lost time testing and retesting, but I never lost money because I never purchased a system from this company. I looked closely at them but decided it would be a better choice to stick with Intel, Corollary, Zenith, and SCO.

I was successful selling these systems to businesses needing more power than a single processor could provide. Many of the software solutions I was developing for warehousing did a lot of processing and needed the central processing unit, or CPU, to be powerful. As one of the better resellers in the Northeast for Unix running on Intel, I was able to get leads directly from the manufacturer of Corollary. I also displayed the hardware as well as other solutions at shows like PC Expo and Unix World in New York. At this point, because technology was hot, a 10-by-10-foot booth would cost about $10,000 at one of these shows, plus all the expenses for carpeting, phone, etc.

Most shows are a waste of time for a small business, not because shows do not produce leads, but because you need to invest time following up with the leads, and for busy business owners this is difficult to do. This is an area where many companies (including mine) failed; very few actually follow up. The things that did come out of many shows were relationships with one or two bigger companies that turned into large orders and long-term customers. The key here is figuring out which are those winners. It usually has to do with whether the contact is a decision-maker (or someone who has the attention of a decision-maker) or not.

A MISSED OPPORTUNITY DURING THE DOT.COM BUBBLE:

In 1995 the Internet was just starting to take off relative to commercialization. This was a new technology I was interested in integrating into my solutions. I had come up with the idea of an online shopping cart. At the time I was traveling to California on a regular basis as the president of Mini-Byte Software working with SCO and NetConnect. I worked with a company in Los Angeles that was in a similar SCO business. We were always talking about working together. In the mid-'90s, I loved California and thought about moving out there some day. When I approached my buddy with the idea of forming a company based around an Internet shopping cart, he thought it sounded neat.

This was going to be my first ever partnership in business. I interviewed a college student my buddy knew who had experience working with HTML. I explained my

> **It is difficult to focus on too many areas at the same time. Sometimes you can miss a good opportunity, just because you run out of bandwidth.**

design of a shopping cart, and the student understood what I wanted. The plan was that we would fund the project, and I would work on the design and project management from New Jersey. Programming was to be done in California and my buddy was going to manage the programmer, to make sure he put in the time and met my expectations. It was a very busy time for both of us. My company was doing well, and I was continuing to build the NetConnect network of resellers (to be discussed later in this chapter). My partner also had a successful Unix integration company in Los Angeles. After a few months, the programmer was not keeping up on the project schedule. My partner had trouble contacting the student. Again, he was also busy running his company. The application was running on the Internet, but it needed a lot of work. My goal was always to get something working well before launch to keep support calls low, so I was unwilling to start with sub-par software.

This was a frustrating experience, because I did not have a lot of time to expend on this new project with everything else I had going on. The college student was busy between school and his social life. My partner was busy running his company. At the time the Internet was still in its infancy, mostly used by technical people and slowly gaining popularity. Even though the shopping cart I had was good, it had a lot of technical bugs that I found while testing. I could not get local support from the programmer in Los Angeles. Even though I thought that online shopping would be important eventually, the Internet was not yet used for this type of business. I knew that if I invested the time needed to make the shopping cart successful, my current business would suffer. So I made the decision to drop the shopping cart and continue with my successful business in New Jersey. This was the first business venture relating to computers and software that I had to stop prior to finishing the product and selling it.

It was a missed opportunity. Two years later, what would have been a competing product to my shopping cart went public for almost $100 million. The other product was not even as good as what I had developed two years prior. I could have cried over the failed opportunity, but I had already sold my business and was working on the next business. Don't get me wrong, I was upset that I had made a mistake and not gone down such a lucrative path, but at that time who knew? We make our technology decisions based on the best available information, our priorities, and our gut. It's OK if we're not always perfect.

DEVELOPING A NEW CRM PRODUCT

By the early '90s, I was looking for the next phase in my growth. I could have kept doing the same business I had been working on for the last 12 years, but I was ready to expand and grow my skills. At this point, I had been working hundred-hour weeks for 10 years. If I had children, I would not have been able to invest this much time in the business. It is important to measure your priorities in life.

By this time, Mini-Byte was no longer selling warehousing software or accounting/business software. I searched for an application that would handle support for hardware and software installations. I could not find anything that was customizable and reasonably priced. I decided it was time for an application to be written that could handle customer relations and track support. I called it "Support Track." It would be used to manage and track support calls and visits to customers.

At that time (1993–1994), Customer Relationship Management (CRM) software was not yet common, but that is essentially what I was developing. What I decided to do was to modify the accounting system I previously sold. It already handled customers, inventory, and orders. I decided that instead of orders it could be changed to track time, technicians, and customers for support calls. Whenever possible, I used code that had already been proven, which is what was done for the majority of this solution.

It took about three months to complete this software modification. The beta site was Mini-Byte Software — I got to use my own product in action before deciding if it was ready for customers. Even though the company was small, our CRM-type needs were the same as any larger company.

> **Whenever possible you should always try to jumpstart a new idea by using existing contacts and relationships. Customers where you already have a history can give you some honest recommendations, and if something doesn't work perfectly they may not get upset.**

At the same time I was the president of a group of the largest SCO Unix resellers (most of them members of the SCO Advanced Reseller group) in the country. These were going to be the perfect companies for using my new software. So of course, I worked to start my new product by offering it to this group. Once built, as long as you have a good reputation you can go back over and over again for business and leads. They also can become resellers of the solution to their customers.

At the annual SCO Reseller show, MBS Solutions (this was the manufacturing side of Mini-Byte Software) rented a table and demonstrated the software 12 times. I sent out demo software to all 12 companies. They installed the software on their own systems to try it out. Within 45 days, I was lucky enough to close 11 of these companies. The software was doing well. My largest installation that adopted the software was based near Boston and had sales of $45 million per year. Their usage included 20 technicians and hundreds of customers. This was definitely my premier company reference site.

Other companies that signed up asked for modifications, which (like the warehousing software) I did after hours. This application took virtually no support from my team, which was important since the main networking system business was doing very well (a part of MBS Systems). I was very involved with NetConnect and creating a market for this product.

Again, like all entrepreneurs, I was faced with a decision. The new product was doing well, but I did not have enough bandwidth (personally) to keep the old business running while marketing a new product. Like all entrepreneurs, I had to make the difficult decision to focus on what works. I stopped selling the software, but I kept supporting it. It is important that you never leave customers just hanging, even if you change your focus or discontinue a product. They need support and you can make money charging for support. They will also remain loyal customers who will continue to update their systems.

A STORY OF TAKING NETWORK CONNECTIVITY SOFTWARE NATIONAL:

As I considered other ways to expand and grow my business, I decided to lean on the deep relationship I'd developed with SCO, as well as new trends in networking.

In the early '90s, there were three major network operating systems: Unix, Novell, and Microsoft. Many companies had two or three of these operating systems in-house and they all wanted to share resources and data. Companies would copy files or transfer disks from one machine to the next. There was a need for a bridge between the operating systems.

Novell was the best networking software available. Unix was the best for database servers and could use inexpensive "dumb" terminals. Getting the two operating systems to transparently speak to each other was an important issue to resolve.

I knew a developer in Florida who had created a software solution that made a Unix drive and printer look like a Novell drive and printer and vice versa. The developer was selling the software direct to end users and resellers. He was a one-man outfit. He was very temperamental, as some developers can be. And he was selling his software, but not enough to make him happy.

Ross Perot (a wealthy investor) found out about this product, recognized how it met a market need, and agreed to fund a company with this programmer. The company received $10 million of investment from Perot. The deal was that if it ran out of money, the business would end — there would be no additional rounds of investment/funding from Perot.

The product worked well, and it met an important market need. Experienced executives ran the company. They paid themselves well (which can be a mistake with a startup and limited funding, especially if they have a stake in the company), built a beautiful office, had wonderful materials, and hired expensive people whom they had already worked with. They thought this was going to be a cash cow. They did a few trade shows and spent a lot of money on everything. In fact, they spent the entire investment and forgot that selling the software was the priority.

> **A common mistake after receiving funding is wasting the money on high salaries and expensive materials not needed to increase sales or production. Compensation for owners should be based on performance. Everyone in a startup needs to be hungry, not comfortable.**

Within a year and a half, they were out of money — there were not enough sales to support the infrastructure. The company was draining money too quickly paying for expenses such as rent, salaries, etc. By the end of the second year, the developer got his software back. No one took home any money other than a high payroll and expensive office furniture, computers, etc. Everyone was fired, and the doors closed. Ross Perot was true to his word and never invested another penny.

I was able to take advantage of this situation. I started a new company known as NetConnect, set up specifically to resell the networking solution from this brilliant but temperamental programmer. He had ownership of the software back in his hands, and I was purchasing directly from him to resell.

During the next two years, I got involved with an organization of Unix resellers around the country. These were the elite of the Unix business world (running on Intel chips), selling more than all the other U.S. resellers combined. I had not met these other resellers in person but knew they would be my first target audience for any solution that would match their business profile.

The market was changing quickly with Novell and Microsoft growing very fast. Many Unix resellers started shifting to Novell and Microsoft. While Novell went after larger networks, Microsoft was struggling at that level in the area of networking but was very successful in the small to mid-sized business market. Unix servers owned the database world. On Intel it was SCO; Sun Microsystems was a major player as well as IBM and others.

SCO, the Unix company I had worked with, decided to go after the enterprise market and used all its resources and money in an effort to gain a foothold in that marketplace. It was hoping to get the database server and companies wanting to migrate off minicomputers. At the time, SCO had more VARs reselling small business solutions than Microsoft and Novell. When SCO changed its target audience, it ignored this large VAR channel. SCO saw the rapid growth of Novell and Microsoft and wanted to be a major player in that space.

It had started to pay less attention to the companies that had great solutions on the Unix operating system running on Intel and had helped SCO become that small business leader. I thought that if SCO starts losing more of the VAR market share, my leads were going to slow down and I would either need to do my own marketing or get my company involved in something new.

I continued to sell the Unix to Novell solution even though the software to connect the two operating systems had to be purchased directly from the developer in Florida (Tom). I had met Tom and had a good relationship with him. Because I was a technical sales person, I was selling more that his other resellers. I could call him, tell him about a bug, test when he said it was fixed, and keep my customers happy. Most other resellers had difficulty working with Tom because he was a temperamental developer and prone to anger (he would always call back and apologize, but it did get some customers upset). Tom did not have much of a business after the failed Ross Perot opportunity, but the product was good and still the best available. Since I had the respect and attention of the best Unix resellers in the country, based on a good reputation and being a part of the nationwide reseller organization, I decided to make a business proposition to Tom.

I talked to Tom about selling his product to other resellers and end users (through my company). The only problem was that if I promoted the product there was no reason why a reseller would not go directly to Tom. I came up with a deal. I would get worldwide distribution rights to sell the software and would commit to paying Tom a minimum quarterly amount whether I sold enough licenses to cover the cost or not. This was a little scary since I had never done worldwide sales of anything — not even nationwide sales. But Tom agreed, and I changed my focus from custom software development and networking to networking Novell and Unix servers. I was now going to have to contact all the main Unix resellers and get them to try and then sell my networking solution.

My core business of selling Unix, servers, and desktops was doing well. With a constant flow of leads, I had a salesperson working the phones along with me being around to help close sales. Because of the core business, I had cash to invest in this new venture without dipping into savings.

I prepared materials and got everything ready to hit the road. As a first step I decided to rent a booth at SCO's main showcase event in California. I was nervous. Everything had to be perfect. I was showing the product to the major resellers and distributors for SCO, Xenix, and Unix from around the world. It was an opportunity to meet many resellers at one location. For my booth, I set up a small network with a Novell server, a Unix server, and a Windows machine. I was the only representative from my company. I had signs made, brochures printed, and off I went. Since I had a small company, I needed to leave everyone else back in New Jersey keeping the current customers happy.

Prior to this new venture, I basically worked all of my time out of the New Jersey office. I had no reason to fly anywhere; all my business was between Philadelphia and Connecticut. The last flight I had taken was in 1982 to teach a seminar in San Francisco on databases. People in my office thought it was funny that I was so nervous to fly. I even dawdled as passengers got on, so that the attendant finally asked me, "are you coming on the plane?"

When I landed in San Francisco, it was unreal. I rented a car and drove along the coast playing songs by the Beach Boys, stopping to stand on a dune overlooking the ocean, and calling the office to make sure everything was good. I decided that I could, indeed, enjoy traveling.

Back to work. Since I was already the top seller of SCO for New Jersey and the surrounding area, I knew quite a few people I had spoken with over the phone. Now I had a chance to meet them in person. I set up my table with signs, computers, etc. I was ready. Attendees came up to my table, where I had everything arranged for live demos.

NetConnect was a hit. I was already signing up resellers. While I was there, I made more contacts. After meeting everyone in the group of Unix resellers, they decided to elect me as the president for the next year. They assumed that with my new product I would probably be talking to everyone on a regular basis. This was an excellent opportunity to increase communications with potential buyers. I could contact them as a member of the group and talk to them about sales.

This show also opened markets in Japan, Germany and a few other countries. By the time it was over, I had at least a dozen new companies that were interested in trying out NetConnect for sharing data and printers between Novell and Unix. Many more interested companies wanted to stay in touch.

One thing about being a small business owner and an integral part of everyday functions is that when you go away, you can never truly be away. Because of this, I would spend late nights working on things going on in New Jersey. In the morning, I would get up by 5 a.m. to make calls and talk to the office. I would write quotes, fax them to customers, and make follow-up calls. CEOs and key players in small companies cannot just leave and forget the world that was left behind.

During the next few years as president of this group, I also built relationships with Oracle, Sybase, Informix, and many hardware companies trying to sell to the group of SCO Advanced Resellers. This was without a doubt the group to market anything that ran on or with Unix on Intel.

IS IT WORTH HAVING A BOOTH AT A LARGE SHOW?

To get the word out I was going to need to do larger trade shows. The first network show was going to be Networld Interop in Las Vegas. This was the largest networking show in the United States, during a very hot time for technology companies (also very expensive). A 10x10 booth for the show was $9,500 plus expenses like carpeting, electric, tables, signs, etc. Because my company had only nine people, I was going to be the only one going to the show. Everyone else would stay behind to finish up installations, build machines, and handle support. This was going to be a new adventure.

> **For anyone needing to take products or heavy luggage to a faraway place, shipping it in a box to the hotel is a great way to get there without carrying everything on a plane. Use FedEx or UPS with tracking and insurance.**

I prepared by setting up a small server and a few portable computers (the ones that looked like suitcases and weighed about 40 pounds). I had about 400 pounds worth of equipment that I was either shipping or carrying with me to the show. I shipped whatever I could to the hotel so that it would be waiting for me and I could confirm it was there.

This was my first trip to Las Vegas and my first really big show. The other vendors were giants like Microsoft, IBM, Novell, HP, CISCO, Lucent, and many others. How was anyone going to find me? Luckily, I signed up for a special startup area off to the side with other small vendors.

> **Collecting or scanning business cards is very important. It is also very important to write notes about interested customers, so that when you or someone else does a follow-up call they can talk intelligently about the customer's needs. Many people make the mistake of thinking they can remember. Assume you won't remember, and take notes.**

As I did demos, I would take a second here and there to ask for business cards. I needed to make sure I could get in touch with everyone who looked at all interested.

I worked hard but had fun. I met a lot of people and many were interested in networking Unix and Novell. At 6 p.m., I was still doing demos. By 6:30 everything was closed down. What a day. I went back to my hotel room to read emails, organize the cards and write more notes on the back of every card about the customer. Because the product was a networking tool and costs started at a few thousand dollars, it was not something I could sell at the show. I wanted to make sure when I called them back I knew something about their needs. Being a small-business owner, I then had to respond to all emails and messages from the day. The next morning, I woke up at 5 a.m. (8 a.m. EST), so that I could call customers, write quotes, and give direction to the technical team.

At the show I tried to get as many people as possible to commit to trying out the software. The networking software had a 15-day expiration for a trial. From the show I closed a few small deals. An article was written in a networking magazine about NetConnect. I set up an evaluation for Mellon Bank and another with AT&T. Their evaluations of NetConnect took a much longer time than other, smaller companies. I did end up closing those sales to departments of some large companies.

Over the next few months I did more shows. I did the big yearly show at SCO in Santa Cruz again and signed up 15 more resellers and a few affiliates. Continuing to build a larger reseller channel was a great plan. We would remotely support the reseller at the installation; they would find the customer and talk them into trying out the software. Basically, if you had a Novell and Unix system you needed NetConnect for file and printer sharing. Because NetConnect worked on Sun Microsystem machines, I took out a booth at a Sun Microsystems trade show in Hawaii and at a large computer show in New York at the Jacob Javits Center. The show in Hawaii went well and I met engineers and management people from Sun Microsystems as well as other potential customers.

Things were going well on all fronts with this new venture. I had found a new building that I could rent for two or three years as a sub-lease from a larger company that moved out. This was a great deal; they did not want the building empty and I wanted an impressive stand-alone building with my own parking lot. Even though I only had nine employees, I thought this 10,000-square-foot building would give the impression of being a larger company.

Partly because I was willing to work 16 hours a day, our company was able to produce great results. I managed complex sales, and I had oversight with the technical support team, project management, order management, and key customer relationships (just like many other small-business owners). I did not do all the work, just coordinated and made sure everything was up to my standards. If I kept the company this size, it was possible for me to manage all these things. I never thought of it as too much; it was fun being successful.

With 10 employees I was able to run a $3.5 million business. At this point I was not doing any programming. The company turned into a computer network, security, and manufacturing company. Mini-Byte Solutions basically replaced many of the minicomputer systems that were sold to the small and mid-sized businesses in the New York, New Jersey, and Pennsylvania area. I still had a great relationship with SCO and we received excellent leads. We were now getting leads from companies that were selling multiprocessor computers, which was one of our specialties because they ran Unix and were great as database servers. The three business units I had built functioned smoothly together. During this phase of growth and maturity, I got to learn even more important lessons.

THE RIGHT FRAME OF MIND TO SELL A COMPANY:

As an entrepreneur, it's important to be thoughtful about what you're learning from your own experiences and to carefully watch the other companies in your ecosystem. Some of the best lessons I've learned have come from watching my customers' successes and failures.

For example, the largest company using my CRM (Customer Relationship Management) software, near Boston, grew to $65 million a year and decided to sell.

> *A more expensive solution is not always the best for your company. Some products are so complex they slow down productivity and time is lost.*

Because of the value of the potential sale, a consulting firm in mergers and acquisitions recommended a high-end accounting system and a high-end CRM / customer support application. At this point there were a few very expensive solutions on the market that cost roughly 10 times what my product cost.

This company chose Siebel, a very high-end product that cost about $600,000 to install and get running. The process took about six months and thousands of hours. After using the product for another six months, my old customer was still having problems with Siebel. It was costing the company a lot of additional money every month. More importantly, it was costing the employees a lot of lost time. They asked me if I could help them set up a way to transfer information back and forth from my system to their new accounting system. This was not difficult; all I had to do was give them an export function and the format of the data.

In the end, my customer dumped their $600,000 investment and went back to my $7,500 solution. Within days the support admins were back to being extremely productive, with no additional costs. I learned how much efficiency matters to an organization of this scale.

I also learned that expensive software is not always the best solution. With my solution, the customer dealt directly with the developer who knew the software inside and out, so anything needed was changed quickly. As a startup for a new business or add-on business, it is important to be nimble and take responsibility for your solution. Our solution was complex enough to handle all the functionality needed, without giving more than what was needed.

> **Selling a company when a good offer is made is quite frequently the best choice; holding out for another offer that doesn't exist yet is taking a big chance. It is important to see where the market is heading before making a rash decision, and remember not to be greedy. Consider everything, including why you decided to sell in the first place.**

This same company taught me another lesson, one that would be useful for me in the future. The owners were offered $10 million to sell their company, but refused it because they thought they could get more. I had recommended the selling of the company, because they had a low profit margin even though they had a high-volume business. They then explored the option of going public, which took a lot of energy and money. They ended up not going public and eventually sold the company for a much lower price when the market was not as hot.

COMPANY SIZE BASED ON YOUR COMFORT LEVEL:

I was the typical small-business owner — very controlling — and felt like I had to micro-manage almost everything. This became difficult as the business continued to grow. By the late 1980s and early 1990s Mini-Byte had 12 employees, doing about $3.5 million of business a year. At this point, there were three parts to the business.

First, Mini-Byte was a manufacturer of custom computers and servers. These were based on Intel single and multiprocessor systems. Companies purchased our servers for a few reasons. If they were purchasing the software to run their company from Mini-Byte, it made sense for them to purchase the entire system from the same company. That way you never got two companies pointing fingers at each other if something was not working correctly. A level of trust needs to be established so that a potential client will invest their future with you. I closed the sales and I was involved in the ordering of parts. A receiving person would record when items arrived. When all the parts were in, the systems would be assembled. At night I would check the work done, and if something needed attention, it would get done prior to the next morning. This was the micromanaging done on the hardware systems. Because it was my company, I handled final quality control.

The second part of the business was selling NetConnect, which was a networking software product to connect Unix and Novell Servers. This was a pure product sale where modifications were not made. There were enhancements done by a developer in Florida (who was not an employee). I was the only person in my company who could sell this software since it was a very technical sale.

In each portion of Mini-Byte, I had a high level of control. This definitely limited my ability to grow, but I was comfortable with a company with no more than a dozen people. It was a personal and business choice. It is important to recognize your comfort zone for control, learn when to give it up if you must, and plan the shape of your company accordingly.

CHOOSING OFFICE SPACES STRATEGICALLY

As Mini-Byte matured, we moved our office location a few times. This was always an important decision for me. Though we were a small company, I understood that our offices were part of customers' first impression of us. Every location would help to create an overall sense of a company that was doing well. This was a time in history where many smaller companies would be here today and gone tomorrow; I needed to avoid the impression that we could close shop any moment.

I always had a training room and a small warehouse in the back with what looked like a great inventory. Again, this was about perception. In today's world, there is something known as "just in time inventory." If you have local sources for everything you need, your materials can be there the next day. You only order as needed, which is far less risky. Keeping significant live inventory was a scary thing for Mini-Byte to do because of the speed at which technology was changing. The newest greatest computer could be received today, and tomorrow a machine 50% faster could be released for the same price. This meant that the brand-new equipment just received dropped in value. To counteract problems like this, I set up multiple vendors with one-day shipping or emergency pickup and ordered only when I got an order.

But all of this could not be explained easily to a customer. So, what do you do when giving a tour of your facility — show an empty warehouse? That is not impressive and does not help strengthen the sense that you are a "real" company. In our warehouse, some of what looked like inventory had computer systems in them already ready to deliver. When we sold a computer, we held the support contract for repair and we kept the original boxes that had the company name, specs and usually a picture in case we had to ship the systems back to the manufacturer (this also took up shelf space). We would leave potential replacement parts that shipped with the system in the box, so they were easy to find. When customers would walk through our location, the warehouse looked like there were many systems available to ship, even though many were actually empty boxes.

I knew that perception of our office space was important, because many potential customers were nervous about whether a small company would survive the next three or more years. I can remember talking to a local company about selling them a complete computer network including a new server. The computer was going to be built by MBS Solutions. At this point, we had already been in business for 12 years and had many great references. But the father and son company was nervous that maybe we would not be around next year, and then what would they do?

The owner's son came to our building to evaluate us. I took him on a tour. I showed him our assembly and testing room as well as the rest of the building. I then had to step out to answer a phone call. Our receptionist overheard him call his dad and say, "Yeah, this is a real company. They have a great building and the owner and technical staff are great." The next day, I received a deposit for a complete system. Six months later, he became a customer I used as a reference. Impressions matter.

> **Perception is very important when selling something to a company that will rely on your solution for years to come.**

Whether it will be software or hardware, you must look like a company that is professional and that is still going to be around in five to 10 years. A two-room office does not instill this kind of confidence. Your office does not need to look like a palace, though. In fact, if it is too fancy, many people will think that maybe you are charging too much money or spending unwisely. A balance is necessary, and professionalism is a must. An accountant can help you decide whether to buy or rent. Usually with a startup, renting a space is much better than purchasing a building, because it is difficult to know what space might be needed at the end of two years and having the cash for hiring and growth is more important than owning a building.

RELYING ON ACCOUNTANTS WHO UNDERSTAND SMALL BUSINESS

Accountants who specialize in working with small-business owners can help you make many choices wisely. For example, my accountant had recommended setting up two companies: one for manufacturing and one for software development. If the two were combined as a single software company that built computers, I could not write off inventory of computers and parts (because it was a service company). Since I had been building computers for many years for resale, the accountant set up MBS Solutions as strictly a manufacturing company, which has a different way of handling taxes and inventory. Once MBS Solutions built the computer for a Mini-Byte Software customer order, the computer would literally be purchased by Mini-Byte Software. What this meant was not paying taxes on inventory meant for building computers.

> **Small business accountants can save you money and keep you from making mistakes that might cause a tax issue. Use professionals so that you can focus on the goal of growing the business and making money.**

Once you grow past a few people and get involved in complex business processes like manufacturing, get a good business accountant involved. He or she could possibly save you money and taxes prior to a product shipping out to a customer. In my case, the business ended up paying taxes only when the system was actually sold to a customer.

As a business owner, you could spend your time learning all about taxes, or focus on growing and keeping your company profitable. I would recommend staying focused. Personally, once I hit a certain billable rate per hour, I knew it was more economical to hire someone to cut the grass, paint my house, and fix my car, while I continued making much more per hour either consulting, programming, or selling. In addition, accountants could understand the tax complexities of running multiple business entities that operated across state lines far better than I ever could. Hiring outside people can make perfect sense when your time is so valuable and their expertise in a specific area is greater than your own.

Chapter 5:
Exit Strategies

Early in your entrepreneurial career, it's easy to focus on starting and running your business, never giving any thought to how the business will end. At the start, you just want the business to be viable, grow, and make a profit. But eventually, you will shift to considering how you can exit your business. Whether you close, sell, or transition leadership, you may find yourself needing to think strategically about an exit strategy so that you can prepare well in advance.

In my case, I had been watching the market and realized that Microsoft and Novell were beating out Santa Cruz Operation (SCO). In the late '80s and early '90s, SCO owned the multiuser small business market. Many companies made sure their software worked on SCO because there were so many resellers and happy customers. But in the early '90s, SCO decided to make a push for the enterprise market and ignored the VARs selling to the successful small and mid-sized business market. SCO spent a lot of money and energy going after that enterprise market. The small business application software vendors noticed this and started shifting to Novell and Microsoft networks. This was the beginning of the end for SCO, and I could see it happening.

At one of the shows I attended, I met some key people from Sun Microsystems. The very first thing I did was to talk with Sun Microsystems about licensing or purchasing NetConnect, my Unix/Novell crossover company. Sun had Unix systems, and NetConnect offered a solution to make Unix look and act like Novell. Sun needed this software; it would drastically increase its interoperability.

NetConnect had one competitor, but the competitor's software was definitely inferior to NetConnect's. It did, however, have investors and was a larger company. NetConnect actually consisted of Tom (the developer in Florida) and myself as salesperson. Sun never asked; they assumed I was a part owner in NetConnect. We acted like one company to all customers, since my company was the only distributor and support center for NetConnect. I was going to benefit from the sale by making a commission, but did not own the product. To me it did not matter.

FIRST A WIN AND THEN A LOST OPPORTUNITY

After showing the software to Sun's technical and sales people at one of the shows, they decided to pay a visit to my office in New Jersey to discuss the purchase or license of the software. I was very nervous because even though Tom was extremely bright, he had a programmer's personality and could say the wrong thing at the wrong time. But Sun Microsystems wanted to meet Tom also. So I arranged everything. Sun and Tom would come to the impressive Mini-Byte/NetConnect office space in New Jersey and hopefully close a deal.

Mother nature did not cooperate. Tom got in the night before. The people from Sun landed in the middle of a snowstorm. It looked like they were going to get stuck; they canceled our meeting and were trying to get a flight out for another engagement they had the next day. Tom was upset and just wanted to go back to Florida. But of course, there were no more planes because of the snow.

He opted to drive to Philadelphia and take a train further south. He headed out without even letting me know. Tom was angry that he came all the way up to New Jersey and Sun was not going to show up. Almost as soon as Tom left, I got a call from the Sun Microsystems visitors, who were stranded and stayed at a hotel that put our office on the path back to the airport. They decided to have our meeting after all the next morning. I was excited to be able to handle the conversation without Tom's volatility. Tom was travelling, and this was before cellphones were common, so I had no way of contacting him.

Four people from Sun arrived in the morning. I took them on a tour of the building (explaining our small numbers with the excuse that some people could not make it in because of the snow). I gave them a live demo on a real network, and everything went well. They needed to speak with Tom, but this looked like the product they wanted to buy outright, and the company looked solid enough from what they could see today. I had to pray that when Tom spoke with them everything would go well, and we would seal the deal.

The first phone call with Tom and Sun went smoothly. They were going to send him a contract to purchase the rights to the software and his services. From there on out, everything about this deal went badly.

Because I was not officially an owner, I was not part of the negotiations. Tom did everything wrong. He told them that he was the sole owner and he would be in charge of negotiations, so now they understood that they were only dealing with Tom. (This might have hurt our chances since they really liked me and the support team in New Jersey.)

They were still interested in Tom the engineer and the software. Then things started going sour relating payment terms. During negotiations, Sun got nervous about dealing with only Tom, who was a one-man development company. Ultimately, they went with our competitor's product, despite it being inferior. Even though they spent $10 million on the deal, the product was never as good as NetConnect.

I was disappointed. I had gotten us to the point of being sold to Sun, but the deal was lost because I had no control. I continued to sell NetConnect since I had the contract with Tom. I learned a lot about selling a business, lessons that would apply when I worked to sell my own company. If at all possible I needed to be in more control of any deal I worked on. This is true for all entrepreneurs considering selling as an exit strategy.

> *Selling your business is the most important sale of your career; it needs careful attention and management. I also learned not to build too much of your future around a person or product who is not part of your team. Not having control of your own destiny is not where you want to be.*

THE SELLING OF A SOFTWARE BUSINESS:

After the sale to Sun fell through, I was in a position to reevaluate the next steps I wanted to take with each of my companies. Like most decisions, this was informed by both professional and personal priorities.

Professionally, I saw a trend in the market away from SCO, Sun, and NetConnect. Since a big part of my business relied on NetConnect and SCO, I decided now was the right time to sell the business (while SCO was still doing well).

Personally, I was re-evaluating my life. I had spent 14 years working hundred-hour weeks. Recently, my mother had passed away, and I was reflecting on the old saying that "no one on their death bed ever says, 'I should have worked more.'" I was ready for something different, and I was ready to cut down a little.

The professional and personal priorities aligned, and I listened to my gut. I was not worried about what to do after a sale. It never crossed my mind, and I knew that I would find new projects. I put the word out that my company, which was one of the highest volume resellers of systems based around SCO, was for sale. As an added value, I owned the exclusive right to sell NetConnect worldwide (which was still a very viable product)

There was a programming outsource company from India with offices in the U.S. and India. The company, called Silverline, was doing well with outsourced programming contracts and decided to start selling products in India. They were selling SCO Unix, Informix database software, and other software products. This did not distinguish them from other companies. So they were looking for something to take to India to sell that would differentiate them from other India-based companies. India was not a wealthy country, and businesses could not afford to put a desktop computer on every desk. This meant SCO Unix was an excellent solution: one server and then dumb terminals or low-end computers on every desk for printing and connecting their Microsoft desktops. Many had Novell, which was superior in managing networks and printing. Just like any company with this combination, they needed the disparate systems talking to each other seamlessly.

Silverline called SCO and asked if they knew any companies with a solution. I received the lead from SCO (lead generation helped me again!) that an outsourcing company was looking to expand its product business in India. They had offices in all the major cities in India. India was a big market for SCO and Novell and they needed NetConnect. I had the solution for their products department, and there was a market ready for this solution. It sounded like an excellent deal.

As a bonus for the Indian company, they would get Mini-Byte Software, which was a profitable Unix and software integration company. They were really mostly interested in the NetConnect for the Unix to Novell integration, but Mini-Byte's entire solution would support their goals. Silverline signed a contract with Tom for the sale of NetConnect and payment of royalties.

Working out a contract with the Indian company was challenging. I came to a basic agreement with the owner, which would have them purchasing my company for 50% down, 30% after 6 months, and the remaining 20% at the end of the first year. I committed to work for the company for two years. I would have to travel to India to give presentations to about 100 companies in five different cities as well as training local sales and technical people.

> **Many lawyers are not focused on getting your deal done; they sometimes imagine issues or get stuck on details that do not matter. You need to stay very involved in all negotiations to make sure they can close. Many gut decisions need to be made, and the lawyers and accountants don't work that way.**

All of this sounded good to me. I found a lawyer based on my accountant's recommendation. This might normally be a good partnership, but in my case, it was a mistake having a lawyer and accountant who were friends. The two got together to talk about the sale of the business, wasted a lot of time talking about other stuff and were not making any progress (while billing for all their time together).

After two weeks of the lawyers going back and forth, it looked like the deal was going to fail. Two weeks prior when I spoke with the owner of Silverline, we had a preliminary agreement. I could not understand why it was failing, since we had a basic agreement and both owners wanted it to happen. So I arranged a meeting with the other owner without any lawyers present. In that one meeting, we agreed on everything and the deal was signed the next day.

The company sold. I received the 50% down, and for the first month everything at my company stayed the same, except Silverline moved one of their management teams into my offices. Other than that, it was business as usual. I had to get a passport since I had never travelled outside the country. I prepared the computers needed to be able to demo NetConnect in India. Everything was looking good.

The local employee who was placed at my location was not very helpful. Part of the problem was the dot com bubble. Many people sat in front of their computers staring at stock market screens, placing orders rather than working. This was an issue with the Silverline employee and a few more executives in that company. The management team should have realized that there was this distraction, which was affecting some of their employees. (Similar distractions exist today with social media.)

Nothing else changed in my office. All employees remained. Nothing changed for anyone in the company, except for me. I was on a salary (as before), but now profits would not be mine, they would belong to the new company. I had Tom flown up to meet the new owners and assured him that I would remain his main contact. He was okay with everything as long as I was involved, and he continued to get his quarterly payments.

The sale of the company meant that all the offices in India were going to sell NetConnect. I was given the job of traveling to India to set this in motion. First I had to prepare a full system to take with me to handle the demos of NetConnect to potential customers and to train sales and technical staff on NetConnect (the systems to take were a Novell server, an SCO

> **When traveling abroad for business and bringing equipment, work with people who can help you through customs. Never leave things for the last moment.**

Unix server, a Windows laptop computer, and one terminal). I tested everything repeatedly before the trip. Most professional people in India speak English, so language would not be a problem. But the cultural and logistical difficulties of doing business halfway around the world were significant.

Flying to India was my first trip outside the continental U.S other than my business trip to Hawaii. I landed in India and immediately learned how different things could be in another country. When getting off the plane I was greeted by a representative from the parent company (who was the brother of the owner in the U.S.). Because of all the electronic equipment I brought with me, customs officials were suspicious. I was shuffled into a room with some military officers. We had a long discussion about what I was doing in India. It was important to note that I had representatives from Silverline who knew the officers with me. After an hour, I was free to leave.

I was taken to an area known as Santa Cruz (what is the chance that the name of this city in India was the same as the city in California with the company SCO!). This was a free trading zone, which meant free of taxes so that they could trade with the U.S. and other countries. I was brought to the main office to train some of the sales people on how to sell NetConnect. Silverline had offices in Bombay, New Delhi, Madras, Calcutta, and a few other large cities.

Everyone in India was very excited. They really wanted their product division to do well, and right now that division was struggling. After a great night of sleep, good food, and clean sheets I was ready to help them. (Just a precaution to those travelling abroad in developing countries: be careful about the food you eat and never drink from a water bottle that was opened before it got to you.)

I set up my equipment in a conference room at the hotel. Things were similar to the U.S. when doing a presentation. Food, seats, a large projector screen, etc. About 30 companies were represented. I demoed the software and basically taught about the technologies. At first you would have thought that the audience was not excited. They were so polite; they just sat there — no questions or responses. I started asking the clients questions about their companies so I could explain how NetConnect might fit. After a while, the audience started responding. When we were done, they applauded, and we shook hands. Ultimately, the presentation got a great response. When I was done, the room was emptied and then filled again with another 30 companies. Same demo, same response. This was going to be very successful. We had banks, mid-sized, and large companies attending.

When traveling abroad for business learn the customs before presenting, don't wait until you get there. Always prepare!

Once I was done, it was off to the airport to travel to the next city. Travelling was nothing like I ever experienced. The cabs did not have enough room for my equipment, so it was tied to the outside of the cab on the roof and on top of the trunk with ropes and bungee cords. I was so nervous that the equipment might fall off and then the shows would stop. Luckily, they did not fall and everything continued to work.

Driving and traffic was different in India. At a light everyone just pulled up, anywhere, including about a hundred three-wheeled taxis, delivery carts, and motorcycles. When the light changed, it was like the start of a race. Everyone would try to be first. If you were on a four-lane road and your two lanes were blocked, no problem, just go the wrong way on the other side, get past the traffic and jump back in.

Delhi, Madras, Calcutta, and others were all on my itinerary. At each city the response was overwhelming. Applause after each presentation. Customers wanting systems set up for trial basis immediately.

I was now going to train the sales and technical people at a conference set up at a resort. People were coming in from all over India. In India in the mid-'90s, there were different classes of people even in the business world. The executives flew, and the others took trains, many of which were crowded and not air-conditioned. So many of the people coming to this meeting were on these trains for 24 to 36 hours. They got there exhausted. This was considered a real treat for them, and the resort was beautiful.

I had flown into a city close by. Everything about this little airport was like old-style movies of Clark Gable flying into a remote location with tons of people hustling around. Then we were tying computers onto taxis again, riding down old dirt roads passing elephants carrying logs and oxen pulling carts. Then I finally got to the end of the road and we jumped on small boats to ride on this very large body of water to get to the resort that was on its own island in the middle of the lake.

The island was a converted coconut plantation. My hotel room was really a little cabin with an air-conditioned room to sleep in and a bathroom. This bathroom really needs an explanation. I opened the door to a courtyard about 25x25 feet. Along the edge was a tiled floor, to the right was a toilet, and to the left a shower. In the middle of the room was a coconut tree with the entire center open to the outside. So going to the bathroom or showering was outside (with a small roof around the outside edge), but everything in the middle having no roof. It was totally private because it was all enclosed. When it rained, and I used the toilet or shower, I would get sprayed with the water coming down next to me. I loved the experience.

I ended up training people in a large hut with a straw roof and bamboo curtains (no windows). Except that it was about 95 degrees it would have been neat. During one of the trainings, we had a thunderstorm and the rain poured in the bamboo curtains. No big deal, we just continued. Most of the people I worked with in India were very laid back and accustomed to this type of inconvenience.

After the sales and technical training all over the country we came back to debrief before departing back to the U.S. I explained to management that each office in every city needed to have a demo network system to learn and test NetConnect prior to installing the trial systems at the different companies. This meant they needed a Unix System, a Novell sever, and at least one Windows desktop machine. I was assured this would happen. After four weeks of demos and trainings, I was on my way back to New Jersey. It had been a great trip, and everyone was psyched. The company knew they had made the right purchase.

But after my trip, things started to go wrong. The systems for each office were never purchased. Every trial went badly — they were on support calls with my staff in the middle of the night because of the time difference. Essentially, they could not get anything to work.

> **If you want to sell a technical product, you will need significant training and installation/troubleshooting time. If this time is not spent prior to an installation, it will probably fail, and the sale will be lost.**

I had demoed to companies similar to FedEx in India and one of India's largest manufacturers. The demo systems set up at their offices did not work. It seemed like my great trip was going down the drain. I recommended to Silverline management that we needed to send one of my technical people to India to get things running and to train the people working for Silverline in India. I sent one of my technicians to India, and every system he touched was working within a few hours. Things were looking up.

Then something unforeseen happened. Because of Y2K coming, Silverline landed a huge deal with a large New York bank for outsourcing as many as a few hundred people in India for programming. Since this was the main thrust of the company and they did not have the resources to handle all this new networking work, they had to make a business decision. Either invest in the product division with equipment, more training, and sales, or focus on outsourced programming services (with no new sales, equipment, or training costs). To them the decision was easy: cut the product division, which had been difficult to get up and running. They decided to drop selling all products in India and focus entirely on outsourcing.

It is important to understand that the new contract they just signed was worth many millions of dollars, and they had to staff up to complete the work. We sat and talked. The Silverline management had made two payments towards fulfilling their contract with me. They made me an offer I could not refuse. They would give me my company back, and I could keep everything they had already paid. No strings, just a clean break. They wanted to focus on their core business, which at this point just took off. Since the contract with NetConnect was now with Silverline, I decided not to pursue that and get it back. At this point I was happy not to have the pressure of trying to build and maintain the NetConnect market.

This was very acceptable to me, since I still had a viable company — along with their first two payments toward the purchase. I was in a unique position: I'd sold my company, made a profit, and still had a company to run or sell again!

SELLING THE SAME BUSINESS A SECOND TIME:

I had a choice to make. Either I could restart my own company, or I could work to sell again. Either way, I had to make sure that Mini-Byte remained viable. My company was down to four people, and one of the technicians was going to stay and work for Silverline running their expanding network. I knew our strength was still in our contacts with SCO as well as our previous customer base, sales, and technical support. I was going to have to hire people, open an office, and continue doing business. Doing all this did not excite me, but I knew what had to be done.

It is important to listen to your instincts. Mine were telling me that it was time to get into something new. I could not imagine keeping my current company where the business was tied to SCO, when I thought they were in a downward spiral. I was ready to move on to learn something new. On the other hand, it is not wise to throw away a company with history that has value. There are many companies in the world that support technologies that have an existing base of clients and new ones still upgrading older systems. Even though my prediction was that SCO would eventually lose to its competitors, it was still a relevant supplier for the small to mid-sized business market. Therefore, doing the work to keep Mini-Byte running made sense, and planning to sell in the near future also made sense.

SCO told another New Jersey company, a competitor of mine, that I was thinking about selling or merging. The owner of that company knew of my track record. This competitor, who became a potential purchaser, was about 30 miles from us. Mini-Byte actually did more SCO business than this purchaser, even though they had 25 employees and I was down to three. Their services business and overall revenue were larger, but they did not have a strong SCO lead business and adding Mini-Byte could strengthen this component of their business.

Instead of offering a cash buyout, they wanted to keep me on to show how Mini-Byte could maintain such high profit margins and help integrate that business into their company. We came up with an agreement where I would make 50% of the profit from the Mini-Byte business division, and I would be paid a good salary to run that division and help this company grow their core business. They were in the process of signing a deal with SAP to sell to the small to mid-sized business market. This was a major undertaking, and my help was needed to start a BASIS installation team. This was the team to install the physical hardware and operating system and to set up the SAP software. It is very technical and could easily cause an installation to fail. I signed a two-year contract to stay and run my old business as well as help them get into this new technology.

Things worked out very well. As I was integrating into the new company, the business of setting up SAP and BASIS installations started to grow. It was difficult at the beginning, with significant complications on the first installation, but we learned from every customer. We developed a process that let us perform installations more frequently and easily, and revenue from that division of the business became significant. At the same time, I was still running the division that had been Mini-Byte Software. The profit margin was high, and that division was successful, too.

Then, a new opportunity arose. Because of the success of the new SAP sales/installation business, a publicly owned company wanted to acquire the newly formed division. They did not want my Unix integration division (which had formerly been Mini-Byte). They did want me as an employee, so once again I had to decide what I wanted to do. Once again, I was offered my old company back for free! I took the company back again and did not go to work for the new company. I also worked out a deal to continue to employ the two employees who had stuck with me for the last seven years, including two cycles of being sold.

My first two exit strategies were failures in the sense that I didn't end up exiting the company. However, they were both very profitable for me, and they taught me a significant amount about the ways that a company can transition ownership. I was ready to try again.

SELLING A BUSINESS FOR A THIRD TIME

At this point in my life, I wanted to figure out what to do next, and running a company with employees was not at the top of my list. So rather than selling to a big company with another complicated deal, I decided to take an unusual route. I worked out a deal with my two employees where they could own the company and just pay me a small amount of the profit for the year. I would help them and not charge anything additional for my services. Even though the Unix integration business shrunk to about $1.2 million, it could easily support a small company and keep my employees comfortable.

At the end of about 8 months, the company had shrunk a little more but was still profitable. I was helping them but not trying to make it grow. It was their responsibility. They had no debt and the future was in their hands. The employees (now owners) did everything they needed to do. They had a nice office and were doing sales and offering great support. I surprised them and told them the company was theirs with no other payments needed. This was now the end of 1997. And, finally, I had exited Mini-Byte.

This last "sale" of my company wasn't just a lesson in exit strategies; it was a lesson in leadership.

> When possible, think of your employees as family, especially if they have been with you for a long time. Employees who work hard for your company really care, and they are rooting for the company to be successful. Employees who stick with you through changes have a special bond with you and your company, and they deserve reward and recognition. If possible, offering a future to your employees, rather than just shutting the doors, is the right thing to do.

Finally, I had exited Mini-Byte and was ready to move on to my next adventure.

Chapter 6:
My next phase

I After Mini-Byte, I was free to relax a bit more and to start entertaining new projects. My grit and desire to succeed were still present but were no longer being applied to Mini-Byte. So, at the end of 1997 when I was contacted by a private group of investors, I was very interested.

The group had found a startup that had a software solution to crawl a network and find every connected device. It could then detect events coming from the found devices. This was a valuable service, and it wasn't being done well by any other company. The group initially wanted to hire me, but I decided to see where the investigation went before accepting money. I decided to volunteer my time to help the investors (and myself) learn if it was a viable idea and if the company was worthy of investment.

The startup, Calvin Alexander, Inc., had five employees, including two very smart, young owners/developers. They had come up with a way of finding what was attached to the network, "anywhere on the network." Their software also had an excellent method of inventorying everything attached. This can be a problem on a large sprawling network in enterprise accounts. Because of regulations, companies need to know that all devices are accounted for and meet security protocol.

As part of my due diligence, I called a contact I had at AT&T to try out the product. AT&T needed this capability to track what was connected to its internal network illegally within AT&T corporate. We brought the software into AT&T, loaded it on the system, and let it do its work. The next day we came back, and AT&T was blown away. It found many more things connected to the network than it knew about. Some of the rouge devices were located in their building — for example, some users had small routers under their desks with personal devices connected.

This proved to me that we had something special. The biggest problem I could see was that the two owners had no idea of how to market the product. They had an employee with a background in HR who was supposed to do sales, but she had no clue how to sell products. I recommended to the investors that this would be a good company to invest in if I were to head sales. I offered not to take any pay except for commission on all my sales. They would reimburse me for expenses, but I would earn no additional compensation without sales. I was not an employee: I was outside sales, marketing, and business development. The owners agreed, and the investors agreed. I laid out a plan for getting more customers to set up beta sites.

With the investment, the company hired a few more programmers and testers. I found more beta sites that would also be potential buyers of the software. Overall the testing was going well, but the completion of the software was not going quite as fast as I hoped. And we needed to get exposure. I recommended doing a few national trade shows, like Network Interop in Las Vegas. This was the hottest networking show in the nation.

The owners were so worried about spending the invested money that they wanted me to cover costs if the show did not do well. I became more nervous about them, now. They did not recognize the need to invest heavily in marketing and sales. In addition, they were not focused on completing the product for delivery. They continually wanted to make it better with more functionality, even though I found customers like AT&T who wanted and needed the current functionality. I had even suggested selling a service with a part of their software until it was complete. They did not want to do this, because they only wanted to sell the complete product. This focus on "completion" was a major mistake, but my hands were tied. I decided to stick with them because I knew the product was something special.

Up to this point, I had not made any money because the owners would not sell the software until it was "done." I was getting nervous that the owners always wanted to rewrite the software to make it do more. They wanted it to be perfect before doing their first installation, but of course software is never perfect; there are levels of acceptability and deliverability. I tried convincing them to sell what they had working at that time. They could sell the software for handling the inventory of what was connected to a network. That filled a need in the industry. I explained to them that if we did not sell the software, they would eventually run out of the investment money.

Ultimately, I decided that if they could not deliver the software, I would try to find a company interested in purchasing Calvin Alexander as a whole and moving it forward. I knew that the tech industry was in a bubble, and I was worried that if success was not met soon, we might miss some great opportunities. So, I changed from selling the product to end users to finding a company that might want to acquire us. I did not initially tell the partners about this.

I found several potential buyers for the company. One of them, Micromuse, had the premier networking analysis software available. They were publicly owned, and after testing the software they said they were interested. Now came the next issue: convincing the two young owners that this would be a great opportunity. They thought that they should hold out because they had the potential to make so much money on their own. I really doubted that since they had no business sense. They came up with an idea of getting a large loan from Micromuse for the licensing of the software. There was a hook that they did not seem to mind: if the software was not perfect they would have to return the loan amount of $10 million. Of course, I would have to give back my commission if this were to occur. I knew that I had to convince them that software is never perfect, and without specific wording, the loan was not the correct solution.

At the next show I had us signed up for, I was able to point out to them that Micromuse was talking to other potential acquisitions. I had them listen to the other conversations. I showed them how there are other competitors. Even though they were not as good, they had money and a big company name behind them. The two owners had many secret talks and decided to sell the company instead of taking the loan (this was a relief).

> **It is important to know when to close a deal, even if conditions aren't ideal. Sometimes even waiting one hour or one day can make the difference between making the right decision or having someone else make it for you. Weigh your options carefully. Decide and don't be greedy!**

The sale was close to being completed. The original salesperson should not have received any commission, as she was not a shareholder in the company. But she said that she had to get a percentage of the deal or would sue. Believe it or not, these two guys were willing to give up the whole deal rather than give her a commission on the sale. They came to me and said that if I did not give up 50% of my commission to her, they would not do the deal.

My decision makes for a very important lesson for those of you reading this story. I had a few choices:
- I could say "no way!" and possibly lose the deal, then begin looking for another buyer.
- I could try and negotiate, which would take time and give the potential buyer the opportunity to make a deal with someone else.

- I could say yes and take a 50% cut on my commission.

It was all up to me. In my gut, I knew this was the only way I was going to make money anytime in the next year. To get the deal done and open an opportunity to move on to something better, I said yes immediately. If I had not agreed, this deal would not have happened, and none of us would have cashed out. I made more than I would have if I'd said no.

The deal happened at just the right time. It was an all-stock deal originally worth $10 million. The stock almost tripled in value, making the deal worth close to $30 million by the time it was all done (because of the exploding stock market). Everyone was happy.

Of course, this was all happening just before the dot com bubble burst. I just had the feeling that these highly valued stocks could not be worth what people thought. I was locked in for six months before I could sell my shares, and I was scared to wait even that long.

I led the way for all the investors and owners in that I decided to sell all my shares the first day after the lockout period. Other than some greedy shareholders, everyone followed my lead in selling their shares. We all averaged getting about $75 per share. The stock had already dropped by 50% to get to this number. There were some greedy people (including the salesperson who received 50% of my commission) who figured it was going to go back up and they were going to make a lot more money. Those who did not sell ended up getting only one-tenth the amount of other investors because of the total crash that occurred within months of that sell date.

This was a lesson that is classic with startups and smart people thinking they could make millions even though they have no idea how to get to that point. The investors were all excited about the deal, because they all quadrupled their money in less than one year. I was comfortable that I guided the owners to make the right decision for all parties involved. The software was never perfect, but everyone got to keep his or her money.

Personal Note: In 2000 my life was about to change. For the first time in my life I was about to become a father, adopting two beautiful twin baby girls. This was going to change my priorities from total business to having a family. I decided that my next phase in life would leave time for raising my two daughters.

NETWORK SECURITY SOFTWARE COMPANY
FROM START TO EXIT

In 2000 I decided it was time to find my next adventure. At the beginning of the summer I went to speak with a partner in a company that had consulting and outsourcing services (three of the four owners were from India and had opened an office in India with programmers). Most of their work was with telcos, and then they decided to get into selling products. (Sound familiar?)

The difference between this company and Silverline was that this company wanted to sell products in the U.S. Because of its current customer base, a natural idea would be to sell network management software. They decided to pick the premier product in the industry from Micromuse. Since they did not have experience selling products, they hired an outside salesperson.

After six months, the sales were dismal. The partner involved in the products division called Micromuse about finding someone who understood the Micromuse product and could sell solutions to new customers for them. That was how I became involved.

After Calvin Alexander, Micromuse had hired me to train their people on the use of the product and how to sell it. I was asked to move to their location and take a full-time position. I refused to move, so I was open to finding something new. That's why Micromuse recommended me to ITS, Inc. ITS wanted me to head up sales and train other people to sell the security software products.

This was still a boom time for tech companies. I joined ITS and found success immediately, selling the Micromuse products and services. Then about four months later, the tech industry fell apart and everything crashed. Companies stopped spending big money, and sales were dismal for everyone. I had been thinking about the security market for quite a while and how it was missing an affordable solution for the small to mid-sized business market. (A small business version of Micromuse products cost $100,000 — too much for many small businesses to afford.)

I explained to the owner of ITS, who was running the products division, that I was comfortable with the idea that I could design a product to compete in the network security market. I had an idea of how to handle events in a totally different manner than any other company, and I was sure that it could be accomplished without a large programming staff. My idea included using an unusual database design to handle the testing of events and what occurs when failure or success is met. I explained that if customers were not purchasing the expensive Micromuse product, it was not worth having me work there, and I was willing to go out and start something new. Pete, one of the owners, understood that the market was going nowhere at the time. He was willing to take a chance with my idea rather than have me leave.

In the past, if I had not already been working for Pete in the network security industry, I would have started a new company on my own. But I had signed a contract with him and figured it would be fun to develop something without needing to worry about running a company, handling taxes and employees, etc. I was given one programmer to start development of this new product. The employee had already worked for ITS prior to this job but had absolutely no experience in the networking area. This was not a problem since I would teach him everything needed to get this product rolling. The plan was that if I could show a prototype working within four to six months, I could get another programmer.

I worked with Rokib (the programmer) and came up with a working prototype in less than four months. I was able to show it to two potential customers, explaining that it was not ready yet. Both companies were very interested, especially if it could save them money over the expensive, high-end products already on the market. I now had two programmers on the project. I gave them the newly designed database layout for our production-level product. The programmers had difficulty understanding my design. They could not imagine how such a simple design could work, but it did. Within six months, we had a product to install as a beta. This was the design that I would eventually turn into a patentable product. Every company that viewed the demo wanted to try it. Within 60 days we had our first small installation. This was a great place to start.

Our competition fighting for this particular market segment had as much as $10 million in investments with as many as 100 employees. Because we were a part of ITS (basically a consultant contract shop), we told people that we had 12 people working in the company (at that time there were actually 55 employees working for the parent company of which we were a division). We could not tell potential customers that it was just a designer/project lead and two developers. The size of our division could make potential customers nervous about our chance of sustainability. As I had done in the past, we had to make the organization appear bigger than it was in order to establish credibility with customers. NetMonSecure did have a lifeline in case of hard times, but it was not needed once orders were placed for the product.

Everyone thought we were big enough. The product did not look or act like it came from a tiny company. I did all the initial demos, either locally in person or over the web. As we started to get more traction, one of the partners of the parent company, Pete, started doing some demos at trade shows, and our exposure grew. We even signed up the Department of Commerce and Mellon Bank as customers. We signed McAfee and Network General as OEMs, which funded our growth. Our competitors thought of us as their biggest competition. Again, they had no idea how small we were because of the parent company ITS.

This was a lot of fun. I got to start an organization, create a product to compete with the big boys, and enjoy successful installations. Because of a changing IT landscape after Y2K, ITS was running into some problems because one of its main customers using it for outsourcing was shrinking. This occurred to many companies that had relied on Y2K for company growth. After Y2K, the world did not come crashing down, and companies started to cut back on fixing or rewriting their software. The tens of thousands of consultants hired were let go. This caused the industry to become depressed, and with the crash of the stock market ITS was not alone in feeling the crunch.

This affected our budget for growth. One of our original exit strategies was to be purchased, and fortunately a new opportunity came up. At one of the trade shows where I was presenting, a company looked at what we were doing and became very interested, not as a customer, but as a buyer of the technology. They wanted to integrate the technology into their product. They also wanted to take my database design and patent the technology, incorporating it into their own solution. This was neat — I had never had a patent prior to this, and to get one in this field was amazing.

The negotiations to purchase the company were tough because of the other owners of our parent company. I helped to negotiate the first deal for the company. Pete was on board immediately. The other owners thought they could get a better deal. Instead, they almost lost the deal and ended up settling for less than the original offer. Finally, the deal closed, almost five years after I was hired by Pete to sell a different network security product, which had now become one of our competitors.

I worked with the new company that purchased us for about a year. During that time the patent was completed, people were trained, documentation was written, and I helped with integration. I decided that I did not want to move to Maryland where the new company was located. I left the company when my work and commitment were completed. The patent is now owned by IBM with Allan Woolway as the sole author.

This was fun, and I learned a lot. It was possible to develop a first-class product on a budget competing against much bigger companies with a lot more capital. The key is to have grit, work hard, never give up, and put in the hours. Put together goals that are achievable even though tough. Additionally, pay attention to opportunities and be prepared to shift strategies when it's in your best interest. Creating a patent is a lot of painstaking work. Selling a company is difficult, especially when there are others involved in the decision. But as an entrepreneur, you can have the chance to do it all.

STARTING A NEW CHAPTER AND INVOLVEMENT WITH NEW COMPANIES

From 2006 to 2008, I continued to work on new ideas, trying to figure out what could potentially turn into a new venture. I talked with some local business owners about what they needed and how I might help. This was the start of my mentoring. Since I was over 60, I thought it was a good time to move for the benefit of my two daughters. We moved to a Central Pennsylvania college town near my immediate family.

In 2009 I moved to Lewisburg, PA. I was hoping that with Bucknell University being in town there would be available programmers who might want to get involved in a new business. At first it was difficult trying to find students to work with. I started by volunteering with some local organizations I met on my own, including a church, the Kiwanis Club of Lewisburg, a local builder, an auto dealer, a catering service, and a physical trainer. I set up these organizations and companies with websites and gave advice about how to be successful by growing their customer or membership base.

Each of these companies or groups had its own issues that needed to be resolved.

- The UU Church of Susquehanna needed a new website that was inviting and told more about what was offered.
- The Kiwanis Club of Lewisburg needed a website to share information and event details.
- A local builder needed a website and a way to register those interested in his business by filling out a form on the web.

- A small used car auto dealer needed a site to display his cars and give information about his company.
- A physical trainer was just starting out and needed help with how to attract customers. We continually revised this over a few years, until the owner eventually was able to make changes himself.

In all of these cases, I learned about what each group or company did, and I helped by improving their web presences. I always listened to what the client needed prior to offering a solution. I enjoyed the process of being a business advisor.

After a while I found out about the Bucknell Small Business Development Center (SBDC) and Bucknell Incubator. I went to some presentations held by the group. The SBDC is basically free for local companies and student-owned startup companies. There was an excellent synergy between the SBDC and me. They needed someone to help with new technology-based startups, and I fit the mold. I thought this was great because I could work with more companies and student-based startups.

Each of the companies I worked with had different needs, and I worked as a volunteer helping them to make decisions relating to company focus, product design, and how to potentially reach their goals. I did not have all the answers and quite frequently I needed to do research to offer the best advice. Many of these mentorship stories are described in Part 2: Stories of Other Entrepreneurs.

I relished my role as a mentor and participant in other entrepreneurs' businesses, but all the while I stayed alert for opportunities for my own ventures. Ultimately, my latest business venture came from an unexpected place: my own shoulder injury.

NECESSITY IS THE MOTHER OF INVENTION

Prior to 2017, I had to start each day with a difficult task: getting out of bed. With a bad shoulder and a bad back, the simple act of getting out of bed can be extremely hard. Some with shoulder injuries end up rolling out of bed to avoid pushing with their arms from a lying position.

This was the case with me. I had been trying to roll out of bed, sometimes with great pain, other times almost falling when my feet slipped on the floor. I needed to find a resolution. I was going to have shoulder surgery later in the year, and rolling out of bed after surgery was not an option. Usually when having shoulder surgery or a shoulder replacement, you are told to sleep in a recliner for a few months, until you have recovered enough to get out of a bed without pushing hard with your arms. It may sound silly, but not even this solution would work for me: the button to raise or lower my recliner was on the side of the bad arm. I couldn't reach it, and certainly wouldn't be able to use it after the operation.

I looked everywhere for a solution. The only things I could find were products to fit on the side of the bed (like a hospital rail), but you still needed to twist your back and use your arms to get up. This did not fit my need. I decided to try and build something on my own.

> **If your product idea fulfills a need for enough people, then check for competitors. Ask others if they could use a similar product. If possible, check whether people are willing to spend money to make their lives easier.**

I realized that whenever I tried to sit up in bed without using my arms, my legs would rise off the bed and I had to try to rock myself out. This proved to be very difficult. But realizing about the legs going up, I thought about when I used to do sit-ups with someone holding my legs down. That was much easier. I decided to design something that could hold my feet down, so I would have the leverage to sit up without using my arms.

If the product went over the mattress, it would be in the way all the time. Then I thought that if I could have something on the side of the mattress to hook my foot under, I could get the leverage to sit up. Great idea! Off I went to Lowe's to buy the items needed to build that hook and get support from tucking it under the mattress of the bed I was lying on.

I put all the pieces together and slipped the mechanism between the mattress and the box spring. I swiveled the top rod out, laid down and tried out my new device. I slipped my leg over the edge of the bed and under the rod now protruding from the side of the mattress. Then I pulled with my foot. To my astonishment, sitting up was easy without using my arms. Just that leverage of having my foot under the rod helped me get up. It solved a problem I had had for many years. I knew the PVC was not the final product material — it creaked and moaned as I sat up — but it worked.

I was so excited that I drove straight back to Lowe's to find metal piping to make my next version. The only piping I could find with the connectors was copper. So I purchased all the piping and then brass couplers that could swivel. I went home and built the new version. Wow, it worked with no creaking. I was so excited.

I called a business associate of mine who had created the Ab-Roller, a very successful device for getting your core in shape. We knew that my first big question would be to identify whether there was a real market for the FootAnchor and how large that market was. How do you decide whether the market needs a product to fill the void of being able to sit up and get out of bed without the use of your arms?

We looked at some Amazon statistics and found that the devices to help someone get out of bed using their arms were selling 5,000–6,000 units per month. With numbers like this, we assumed there should be a market for getting out of bed using your foot. We talked about how it might be worth having both a foot solution and one for pushing with hands. This way my new product would have an advantage by offering options for different types of injuries or surgery.

The next step was to build a more formal prototype. I needed to have CAD drawings for any machine shop work. I called a friend who is a mechanical engineering professor at Bucknell University. I offered him a 10% stake in the company to help with many things including CAD. Offering a piece of a company is complicated when creating an LLC, handling finances, etc. I was not asking for Nate (the professors name) for any money to pay for expenses.

Nate was excited to be involved in a startup and I was excited to have him. Our goal was not to burden Nate with any investments or expenses relating to the start of the business. I worked with a lawyer to come up with a contract that would give Nate 10% of all profits and 10% of any event that caused the company to make a profit. Nate ended up with 10% Phantom Shares of the company (in the glossary I explain Phantom Shares).

Finding a manufacturer to help build a working prototype was not an easy task. Companies don't want one-off jobs. Eventually, I found a family-owned machine shop in Huntingdon, Pennsylvania, that would do a one-off prototype. I worked with a Bucknell engineering professor to create the CAD drawings, and I gave the drawings to the machine shop.

The base was designed to be a tubular structure. The only problem was that it was difficult to find companies that could bend 1-inch steel tubing without crimping it. So when I had the machine shop try bending the tube, it was a job that was going to have to be done by hand, which was going to be very expensive. I decided to look into a different solution for the design. I started on a design for a new prototype with a wood base and steel for the swivel and anchor. We had to design it so that there was enough clearance for the swivel to work without having too much play. This was tough without having it built and being able to test it. We decided to have two prototypes built with different clearances. Because of the complexity of the swivel, it had to be built by hand (increasing the cost). The base metal that held the tube in place and connected to the wood base could be cut using a laser CNC machine.

The wood base was being made by a local lumberyard with a CNC machine. This meant they could take a larger sheet of wood and the machine would automatically cut it into the correct size pieces. Some parts were ordered from China and others from parts manufacturers in the U.S.

Once the metal pieces were completed, we decided that they looked dull and the welds were too visible. All the metal parts were sent to a company that does zinc plating. This made the metal pieces look nice but affected the

> Sourcing materials for any new product is an issue. Make sure to allow for the time and expense so you end up with the best solution.

smooth swiveling of some of the pieces. A decision was needed: make all pieces shiny or keep the smooth swivel? The process of learning about manufacturing and the design tradeoffs involved in creating a new physical product was fascinating to me.

Ultimately, the FootAnchor was made up of a few elements. There is a base that tucks under the mattress and on top of either the bedspring or the platform. The edge of the FootAnchor has a rod that rises vertically from the base along the side of the mattress. At the top of this vertical rod is a swivel with a padded extension that can be adjusted to sit perpendicular to the mattress, sticking out from the bed. This "anchor" is so that you can place your foot or ankle under it and use it for leverage to sit up over the side of the mattress. The height of the anchor can be adjusted by unclipping the rod to make it higher or lower, adjusting for the height of the mattress and the length of the user's leg.

Now there was the issue of cost. Small quantities cost approximately $80 to complete. This would mean a retail price of at least $175. If a dealer were involved at a 50% discount, it would be just over break-even. The key was to get the volume up. Even with U.S.-based manufacturing, at higher quantities the price would drop $10 per unit, which would mean either making more money or lowering the price and selling more products. There were many tough decisions to balance.

The price was still too high for the market. The only option was to try getting the FootAnchor manufactured in China or some other country.

At the same time, I needed to arrange how users would find the product and make payments. There are many ways to set this up. I decided that the Square payment platform would be best for FootAnchor, LLC. We were able to link our own storefront on Square.com to our website. Customers could log in and place orders, and their credit card would be charged. The full amount minus about 3% fees would be deposited directly into the company's bank account. We would also get a Square unit to carry around and take credit cards in person.

The FootAnchor was in many ways more difficult to launch than previous tech products. For the FootAnchor I was relying heavily on other manufacturers making my custom pieces. In a technical programming environment, I could just put my head down and turn out some new code to finish a product. For someone like me who wanted to control the entire process, this was a very different and difficult experience.

Things were finally falling into place, except for one thing. I contacted the company that made the anchor, the swivel, and the base to confirm that their earlier quote was still valid. Unfortunately, they changed their mind and, even at larger quantities, were not willing to manufacture the FootAnchor for a price that would let me hit my goal sell price. What to do? My plan just hit a major setback.

Immediately I went back to the drawing board to come up with new ideas for a more affordable way to manufacture the FootAnchor. My engineering partner and I developed specifications for a nylon version of the product. The base unit could be made out of polypropylene. With the latest CAD drawings and specifications, I went to a plastics company for a quote. It ended up that the nylon version would be more expensive than metal. At the same time, I contacted a Chinese company that already made swiveling components for other applications. I asked if they would be willing to modify their products for my application.

The ongoing challenge of pricing and manufacturing was still happening for the FootAnchor. After considering the above options, I decided to get quotes for a bamboo base from China. I had also contacted another company to see if the pricing for making the FootAnchor pieces would allow me to sell at a lower price point.

Based on all of the design modifications needed, it was back to the drawing board. We decided to come up with a design that did not need any welding and was designed using aluminum pieces connected to a bamboo board. The bamboo board would be extended at one end to eliminate the metal base plate. The new design was completed in September of 2018. With the modifications and using companies in China, costs would be reduced by 60-70%.

After discussions, a deal was completed with the Chinese company making the bamboo boards and the prototypes were beautiful. A different company will be handling the remaining pieces needed for the assembly.

Once the final order is placed for all assembly parts, FootAnchor, LLC will prepare a KickStarter campaign, and start marketing the product.

This is still an ongoing process, like many stories of entrepreneurship, it's not yet clear how this will end.

From my early days as a teacher to my latest ventures, I've been fascinated by how businesses work. And I've had the grit to see projects through, even when faced with significant challenges.

In my most recent work as a mentor, I've come to realize how much early-stage entrepreneurs can benefit from hearing stories of what has — and has not — worked for others. That's why I've told my story here in such detail. And it's why, in the next portion of this book, we'll look at the experiences of other entrepreneurs.

Part 2:
Stories of Other Entrepreneurs

Chapter 7:
Students Selling to Students

When I began working with the Lewisburg SBDC as a mentor, my first introduction was to a Bucknell student startup company. They came up with the idea of giving college students the ability to sell items to other college students. This was going to be mostly local, within a college campus, making it safe and adding value since you could pick up an item on the same day. Imagine breaking your phone and finding a used one for sale by someone on campus, picking it up and being back online within hours. Other uses could be for clothes and furniture.

The idea was good, but there were many flaws. These students were describing a large project with many caveats. By the time I met them they had already tried two different programming firms and blown through almost $20,000 in funding. They still had about $7,000 left. The students felt they had met with failure. After looking at what had been accomplished and the fact that the second consulting firm was no longer responding to requests for updates, I met with them for some serious questions.

> **At some point in your life you will fail; if you don't fail you are not even trying. Be open to risk and reset your goals to pursue the dream!**

I asked them if they were willing to invest a lot of their time in making this a successful company. I was assured, "yes!" even though they were considering giving it all up because after a year it had not gone anywhere. I asked if I could lay out a plan using only what money they had left in their budget. They were skeptical — they could not understand how it could be done for under $7,000 — but wanted to try. None of the participants wanted to fail such a high-profile attempt to create this company (everyone on campus knew about this company and what they were trying to accomplish).

I explained to them that what they were actually describing was a site similar to eBay. They could not just sell a product like a normal company; they wanted to set up each student as a vendor using a shared customer base. Each vendor would need to have its own inventory and customers, sell its own products, and track its own activity. This could not be developed on the budget they had now (or even the budget they'd had at the beginning of the project) unless we started with a software solution that brought BuckSell part of the way to completion. I offered my services free as a volunteer mentor.

The entire team of 10 students was excited. We arranged to meet the next week. I researched open source shopping cart / inventory solutions. I located an open source shopping cart and found an add-on to the shopping cart that would give it the capability of making each student a vendor with his or her own inventory. I then located a company in the UK that specialized in the open source shopping cart software. We would use the UK company to host our solution and install it on that company's server. I was ready for the next meeting.

We had about a dozen people show up. I presented what I found and offered to coordinate and create the specifications for the consulting companies. I built a front end for the product and a website for the company. Even though we had students from business, marketing, and engineering, they had no idea where to start. I gave them direction and told them that I should have the site up in about four weeks. I told them we could keep the project under the $7,000 they still had left in their budget. We were moving forward, and the students were not going to fold.

I invested the next month, full time, on this volunteer project. I considered it a challenge. To create a site as described in four weeks is not an easy undertaking. I delegated some parts of the project relating to getting inventory products together to sell, taking pictures, and preparing for entering into the software. We purchased the add-on and hired the company in the UK for installing the open source software on one of their servers, following my specific modification instructions including the integration of the third-party add-on. I worked on the front end; they worked on the back end. I was available anytime they needed me. Complete dedication was needed to meet the strict deadline I set for the first version to be up on the web. I met with the students every week to go over progress. There was a core of about four students who were truly willing to help. But even they were tentative because of the two bad previous attempts to get the software completed.

By the end of the four weeks, I showed the group a running beta version. We were under their budget of $7,000. They were so excited that it made all the hard work worthwhile. They now understood how their site was to function. It was truly very similar to an eBay. Now it was their turn to get work done. The students needed to now show the passion and grit needed to make the product successful. Getting it to run was only step one. This was going to be a great learning experience for these students.

The upcoming work included a few stages. The group needed to solve technical problems and business problems.

Technically, they needed to:
- Allow students to sign up as vendors to sell their items
- Allow vendors (students) to load pictures, descriptions, and prices for their items
- Enable other students to use the site and look up items to purchase
- Enable students to place items in a cart, then purchase all electronically
- Track everything with the software

From a business perspective, they also needed to:
- Develop and execute a marketing plan
- Create a business strategy
- Solve business administrative problems
- Work at making this a success at Bucknell

One group came up with the idea of a pizza party to get students to sign up and either use the site looking for items posted by other students or list their own items for sale. Flyers were made, but the event did not pan out as hoped.

It became obvious that marketing this product was a difficult task. For some reason, getting these students to understand the benefit was difficult. It is difficult to say why the students at Bucknell were not interested in selling or purchasing on the system. One hypothesis was that because most Bucknell students come from financially stable families, they had no need to purchase used things.

From my perspective, there was one other ingredient missing. The company did not have that one dedicated person who would give everything for the company. No one was watching the ship and making sure that everyone else's tasks were happening. BuckSell needed a student CEO to lead the company – someone who was personally invested in the company and its success.

Every company needs that leader — no exceptions. It is a difficult thing to get an application up and running unless someone is coordinating all aspects of the company. I was still handling the programming side, but we needed someone to focus on sales, signing vendors up, and getting students to post items. Without that leadership from within the group, success would be very difficult.

I came up with the idea to get the retail establishments downtown to offer special discounts with a coupon which was being offered only on the BuckSell site. Everyone in the group meeting thought it was a good idea. Yet no one volunteered to go downtown to sell the idea to the merchants. The student who started the company assigned the task to a friend. The problem with this is that if someone does not really want to sell something, it will not happen. The student went downtown and spoke with four retailers with no success. Even though they were being offered free advertising to bring customers to their store, they said no.

I knew something was wrong, maybe just the approach or what he was saying. I put together a script for the student representative. I felt a push back, so I asked if he would like it if we went downtown together. Yes — he wanted as much help as he could get. On a Tuesday morning, we went downtown. We waited at each location for the manager. If not available we found out the name and hours they worked.

When we did get the right person we said, "How would you like to be listed on our site, which is free to all Bucknell students and faculty? We could list your company; all you need to do is offer a coupon for coming to your store. If they don't come, it does not cost you anything. If they come, it is to purchase something." Every retailer said yes. After the eighth store visit, the student got it.

> It is difficult for students to make the decision whether to focus on a business or to put a college education and graduation in the back seat. Without that one dedicated person, a new company does not have a great chance of being successful.

So, was this a success? Yes, on the day we went out. The only problem is the student was busy doing other things and never went out again. Because there was no CEO coordinating things, no one was accountable to track how the visits were progressing.

Then another idea was brought up. At the end of every year, all the students leaving for the summer would put great stuff out on the curb, and local residents would go around scavenging. I recommended instead, why not offer students the ability to offer products on BuckSell, and any money made would go to charity. Again, the problem was getting any students to really commit, which appeared close to impossible. Users of the site were hesitant, and in my opinion, it was because the leaders of the group were not committed themselves.

The organization eventually folded — mainly for lack of that single driving leader, a person with grit, who would see the project through.

Chapter 8:
Measuring the Entrepreneurial Spirit

In the spring/summer of 2014, I was working as a volunteer mentor to a company that had seven partners working to come up with an assessment to measure the entrepreneurial mindset. This was a really cool idea, and the team was made up of a combination of people ranging from very successful business people to long-term educators. The team had an abundance of very smart members.

The company was formalized in August 2014, creating the official LLC in January 2015. Originally the company had a partial version of the assessment running using Qualtrics and it could not handle one of the modules. Qualtrics would have been expensive and not practical for our potential customer base. I convinced the group that they had to move forward and actually create a version of the assessment online where we would own the code and platform (similar to a test format). One of the members who taught engineering agreed to take on the programming part of the project. I helped him to get started by recommending the database and programming language. This was a very big undertaking for one member, who would not be compensated for his work; I don't think he initially realized how much time and effort this would take.

I did not understand who the market would be and whether the company could make any money. It would take a major effort to market this solution. Part of what made this product so different were the questions being asked and the neuro-cognitive section of the assessment.

The members thought that I added a lot of value to the company on the software business side, and they liked that I had experience running smaller technology companies. I agreed to become a member because I respected the other members and really enjoyed their company.

The members had agreed at the beginning to run the company on a shoestring budget. The only real costs were for outsourced programming and web-based expenses. The company joined the Lewisburg Bucknell incubator

> **It is important for entrepreneurs to understand the tax breaks that local and state governments may offer to new businesses in any state.**

(part of the Bucknell SBDC). This gave us a place to hold meetings and an address. The company formed an LLC. Part of the reason for this was to take part in the KIZ program (Keystone Innovation Zone (KIZ) Tax Credit Program), which gives tax credits back for companies that are growing and making more money each year. The main purpose of KIZ is to support companies that hire more employees by rewarding them for increasing sales.

We were on track to get our first online working assessment running in December 2016. Other than the outsourced programmers and the one member who took charge of development, the other members worked part-time trying to locate potential customers for taking the assessment. A few of the members worked on creating the documents needed for a patent. For development of the web-based assessment, we originally started using an outsourcing company based in Europe, with an office in the U.S. But after a few months of sporadic programming and poor communications, we decided that this team was not going to get the job completed within our budget. The money spent on this engagement was lost.

We decided to find another outsourcing company to do the programming. We found one in India and tried their programming skills by giving them small projects to complete. We evaluated each programmer working on our project

> In every programming job, decisions must be made. Sometimes, cutting the cord and breaking away from a losing situation is the correct path.

and told the company when someone was not working fast enough or did not understand what to do. After about a month, we found the right combination, and over the next six months we had a completed project.

EntreMetric was lucky that the one member dedicated himself to getting the programming job done. During the development, there were a few issues such as formatting a PDF from data in a Linux environment. The programming team was stuck for a few weeks on the PDF formatting. We had to do our own research and find consultants to help us. It's important to remember that sometimes it is worth the high cost of an expert consultant, if the advice will save your own team days or weeks. We did find an expert in the field, and in less than an hour he described to us what needed to be done to get the PDF to print correctly.

We did not have a dedicated person to market EntreMetric. I still liked the company, but I was unsure when or how it was going to make money. During the fall of 2016, an interim part-time CEO was brought in with a deal where if end-of-year sales goals were met, he would be offered a 20%

stake in the company and a base salary. The CEO was also going to work part time, since he was already involved in a few other companies. The members of EntreMetric came up with leads for potential licensing deals for the CEO. One of the members who has many contacts coordinated sales activities and meetings as well as bringing in leads. For some meetings the CEO and members of the board went to the client meetings, trying to convince them to license the EntreMetric assessment.

The application was always being modified to give it more functionality. There was a point where I started raising the flag to point out that the product worked; we had produced a good report displaying the Entrepreneurial Mindset and we needed to stop making changes and just sell. Making changes meant that we had to continue to test each new function and pay for the programming. We did eventually stop enhancing the product, which took the pressure off the CTO, who spent more time working than any other member.

In October of 2015 we filed for a patent-pending status based on our unique assessment. Over the first half of 2016, the assessment became better and better. The company decided to validate whether the assessment really pointed out which users had that entrepreneurial mindset. EntreMetric had over 800 people take the assessment — 400 classified themselves as entrepreneurs and had been in business, and 400 had no entrepreneurship experience. This was used in helping to develop the results. EntreMetric used a service to find the experienced entrepreneurs and non-entrepreneurs.

By September 2016 the company had only one sale to a local SBDC brought in by one of the members. Other companies liked the idea, but no one had stepped up to purchase the product. The CEO was still part time and responsible for sales. He did bring a few interns who helped to produce very professional marketing collateral.

Up to this point, the members had contributed the money needed for programming, attorney fees for the patent, accounting services, and database/web costs. The next big expense would be the actual final patent. This patent was the potential key to making some licensing sales. There were universities and businesses doing things similar to the EntreMetric patent. This could potentially yield licensing deals. The first university to discuss this with would be one of the Ivy Leagues. Then there would be others. While working on this there was a possibility that some government / college agency might offer to purchase the entire company and the patent.

One of the members had great contacts at a local university, which turned into a licensing deal once they learned what the assessment produced.

With the potential for licensing from the patent, there was a chance for some income or the sale of the company. When I joined the company, I always thought that the best plan for this company would be to build and prove the product, get a patent, then sell the company or license the patent.

The members of this company never realized how hard it would be to sell the assessment and how much work it would be to get clients. One of the major reasons the sales were not more successful was because there was never a full-time commitment by someone working for the company.

As of September 2017, after being around for almost three years and incorporated for one, the future looked like a possible licensing company.

It actually took some convincing for the members to understand that a sales opportunity report needs to include a gut feeling of whether a lead might have a chance of closing, the percentage likelihood of it

> **It is important to be honest with yourself whether a potential opportunity could turn into a sale. Remember that a sale is when you get a physical order, not just a verbal discussion.**

closing, and when. Without any of this, it is impossible to figure out a budget and impossible to measure whether there is any success in the sales strategy. After getting this report from the CEO, it was easy to see that although contacts were being made, there were no sales ready to close. The CEO did not really want to have a report such as this, but created one when requested by the board.

Did the company end up where I thought it would be? Pretty close. I did not become part of this company for the money. I really liked the members and still do. They have all been successful in their lives. Getting the product completed was a dream of the team. Selling it was not something any of them wanted to focus on full-time; they were all content with their current lives. So, one goal was reached. The future still might hold some licensing agreements and could lead to a profit, but it looked like a tough road. There was also the possibility of using a decision tree knowledge base to help people taking the assessment to get advice on what to do based on their results. There is also a potential to sell consulting time for follow-up to those interested after taking the assessment. This consulting would need to be done by an experienced businessperson.

> **When developing a product, there is a point in time where you need to say it is complete and it is time to start selling. Every product can be better; why not sell now, and release an update later.**

Why is this adventure included in this book? There is a lot to learn from a company that never had a real plan for some of the key things needed to succeed. You need a game plan from idea, to implementation, to building a team, to sales and execution, and you need at least one full-time champion selling and representing the company.

You can always find more enhancements to make, but until they are needed to increase sales, just focus on sales. Never try to start and grow a company without a dedicated CEO (or president or just one key player with no title).

As of August 2018, EntreMetric still does not have a CEO. There was a potential opportunity for an investor, but it fell through. The next opportunity might be selling the company to a firm that needs the EntreMetric assessment to complete a current offering (which

> **Every startup needs at least one person who dedicates his full energy to growing the company. Without that key person, it is unlikely that a company will succeed.**

includes a consulting back-end). Updates about this story, and others in the book, can be found in our online community.

Chapter 9:
To Restaurant or Not?

Highland BBQ & Catering started with a couple who were both working full time and had a small catering business on the side. The business revolved around BBQ chicken, ribs, and other American comfort food. They made potato salad, coleslaw, and everything else in their basement.

When they decided that they wanted to quit their jobs and open a restaurant, they went to their local Small Business Development Center. The SBDC recommended that they speak with me.

After our meeting and conversation, I made some recommendations. The first was not to quit their jobs. The second was to grow their business in a different way from what they had planned: not by opening a restaurant, but by expanding their catering. Opening a restaurant requires complete dedication — very different from working part time and having income for taking care of everything.

I recommended the following: build the catering business so that it could almost replace one person's salary. I offered to build them a website (for free; I work as a volunteer). I also asked them if they attend any functions. They had said no, most of their business came from their church and attendees.

I told them to apply to get into a BBQ competition coming up in Lewisburg. We had their site up and running before the show. I used Wix to set up the site so that the family could easily manage it. We also prepared business cards and other materials so that they could market beyond the narrow circle of their acquaintances.

The competition was a success. They sold out everything that they brought and came in third overall. Building on the momentum they established there, the business started to grow. Sometimes, a single event can provide the motivation you need to prepare to grow, as well as the publicity it takes to earn more customers. At this point, I told them to contact me if they needed anything.

After about a year, business had grown enough that they decided to open a restaurant. This was going to be a full-time life commitment. They worked a lot of hours. The restaurant was very nice and initially successful (because it was new and there was publicity). However, they faced a significant challenge: location.

The building they took over was nice, but it was not on the main street in town. They had a sign with an arrow pointing to their location, but in a highly walkable college town, it's beneficial to be on the main drag. Their sign didn't attract enough business, and the restaurant lost money. Ultimately, they chose to close the restaurant rather than continue losing money. Thankfully they still had the successful catering business to fall back on.

Opening a restaurant is difficult. Jumping into a full-time business can be a mistake, especially if done too early. Make sure you have the finances and some income coming in that you can live off of. Make sure you have built a clientele that will follow you to the restaurant and keep coming back.

Make sure that you remember one of the first rules of retail: location, location, location! Saving money by being off the beaten track will kill a business. If you do not already have a following, do not open a business where people can't easily see your storefront. If not in the line of sight, you need to proactively get your business's name out there.

Chapter 10:
Making scheduling work

Scheduling college courses is notoriously difficult. One of the young entrepreneurs I worked with in Central Pennsylvania had developed an app to make scheduling easier (he was a student at Bucknell). He hoped to turn his app into a business. Like most entrepreneurs, his journey was full of challenges.

Once the app was ready, his friends used and liked it. Through a coincidence, he obtained an email list of the entire student population at his college. At that point, many students tried out the software and liked it, and the entrepreneur thought that he would be able to turn it into a profitable business.

The problem was that the app was only useful at the beginning of a semester. How could he reliably monetize something that was only useful for a few weeks a year?

> **A key question for this product and many others: how can it be regularly and reliably monetized?**

The student decided to try connecting with Amazon to earn commission on new and used textbook sales. That improved things slightly, but still his income was limited to semester beginnings. In addition, students didn't realize that it was possible to purchase books through the system. While the entrepreneur had good fortune with the email blast, he didn't have any ongoing marketing plans.

His next attempt to monetize the app was to offer it to other colleges. He worked to develop routines to incorporate scheduling data for additional schools. But again, without marketing he didn't have a reliable way of getting the word out and encouraging others to try the app.

Through all of this, the student also faced limitations from the design of the app itself. Even I thought the software had an old feel about it. It looked like a text-based app with no graphical interface. Users said they liked it but agreed that it looked like an old mainframe application.

Even in the face of these challenges, the student was passionate about his application and making it a success. The student also had grit.

He was willing to put in all the time needed to make the application a success. The only part missing was a good plan for how he would make money with the product. This is where we worked together. I personally did not think that selling the books for this short period each year would bring in enough. He had come up with a plan that if he could find a champion at another college, they could make money by getting a commission on books sold. I explained to him that I did not think that would work, because even at his own school, where everyone already knew him, he was hardly making any money from selling books. So he continued to explore other avenues for monetizing the app.

For the student, graduation was coming up rapidly. He spoke with his grandfather who was willing to invest up to $100,000 to make this into a product that could be successful. The student decided to take this opportunity to give his product a robust graphical front end and a real-time database backend. I still stuck by my evaluation that making money and getting other college's students to adopt this product would be difficult, though I was impressed with the student's dedication. I thought licensing directly to colleges might be an opportunity. I also knew that the experience this student was getting from developing a complete application in a newer design would benefit him in the long run.

I helped in making a few decisions about outsourcing some of the programming and the type of database to be used. After graduation he put all of his time into development. In the process, he learned how to vet developers and select one who would work well for the project.

The new application took about four months to complete and test. It was beautiful. Then he tried getting some other schools to use it — still without a strong business plan or marketing. He had friends at other schools, but it did not take off. Overall, his grandfather ended up spending about $40,000.

The good news is that because of his experience, he was able to land a great job. His resume included complete development and testing of a product using offshore outsourcing. This was an accomplishment for such a young graduate — thankfully his grandfather agreed!

Even though the product was not a success, the student himself was. His grit and hard work paid off. And he learned a few essentials of app development:

- When developing an application, it is important to project how much money could potentially be generated to create a profit.

- It is just as important to test the waters and see the viability of being able to get customers to grow the business.
- Make sure that if family members are investing their money, they can afford losing the money in case the company fails (you never want to hurt family relationships because of lost money).

Chapter 11:
Products That Stand Out From the Crowd

At a local SBDC event, I met a woman who had already started a company. She was a designer of clothes and accessories —specifically compact and foldable products that can be carried over the shoulder. At the time we met, she had designed a backpack that had a main compartment and a bolt-on smaller piece that could carry part of the load.

The concept was easy and fun: instead of carrying around an entire backpack once you get somewhere like school, put the larger base in your locker and only carry around the smaller pack with what is needed for that portion of the day.

The next product was a raincoat that folded into a small pack that could be carried over your shoulder and hold other things inside of it. A third item was a convertible blanket with one side being soft and the other side waterproof. The owner was also developing a sport shirt that had elastic to put pressure on certain areas of the body, helping to reduce fatigue. She had worked with a local university on the science side of the workings of the shirt.

The first few versions of each piece were all hand sewn. When she first came to me she had found a local company to manufacture the backpack, but only in very small quantities. And you know what small quantities mean: not fast and not cheap. Her company, Pelagoz, was more like a boutique company using a local manufacturer. It may have been a good place to start, but it was way too expensive for mass production.

The owner decided to try placing the products with local vendors, but she still didn't have a plan for marketing. One store accepted her products. The store was a children's store and the blankets did sell. The backpacks, however, did not. The follow-up was not aggressive enough and the store never took a second order, even though the blankets sold.

So what to do from here? I had been recommending that the owner continue teaching while trying to build this business. The business had been moving very slowly even with an online website. She needed her teaching income to live on, and she didn't have a plan that was well defined enough to take the leap into working as a full-time startup.

A company such as this is in a tough predicament. The owner did a great job designing a few products and getting them manufactured. The products ended up costing more than the competition because of using a local manufacturer. Because the owner did not have enough financial resources to work full time on marketing this product, it has not moved fast enough to earn a living. So deciding on what to do is difficult. Finding a buyer for the company and products was difficult because there were so few sales.

> If you are coming out with new products, make sure you have a marketing plan or a sales channel already set up.

Just putting products or a company on the internet does not mean anyone is going to find it. Find stores or others who will help sell your product. With social media there are ways to let people know you have products, but it means a lot of work using Facebook, Google, Twitter, blogs, Pinterest, and many other available resources.

One of my recommendations was to find a company that manufactured products similar to Pelagoz. Maybe it would be interested in the manufacturing side, and the owner could concentrate on creating new designs for which she has a great talent. Not everyone can come up with ideas, design a product, and handle all the manufacturing and marketing. Sometimes it is worth taking a royalty and focusing on what you enjoy.

> If you find that something sells in a specific type of store, then go after that market. Indications of marketplace success are invaluable, and they can help you build and expand.

Chapter 12:
From Database to Product

BulletinCloud was based on an idea I had about a multi-dimensional database structure. The idea was to have a graphically oriented database application. The end result was similar to Pinterest, but with a deeper and more robust structure and content control.

As with other applications I had developed, I knew that if some open source routines were used, it would make the graphical interface much easier and faster to program. The database was a design similar to one I used in my earlier patent. It gave me the ability to control many levels of data that were all related to each other. Within the application you could build Categories and Categories within them to build on the hierarchical data tree. Categories of information could have password protection, and groups could be given permission. If a tile (sub-category) had an expiration date, it would disappear when the date was reached.

I worked with a student developer to create this product, and the story illustrates how a team that is not fully committed to the product can threaten its commercial success. At the time I was mentoring a student at Rochester Institute of Technology (RIT). The student was already programming but had not worked on any full database applications. The student was working on this part time. I was passionate about finishing the product following my original design.

The student took an internship with Microsoft, which meant development stopped during the summer of 2015. This was okay with me since I was involved with EntreMetric and mentoring at the time. At this point the product was not fully functional.

As of the writing of this book, BullitenCloud.com is still unique, but the programmer was hired by Microsoft and cannot complete the application, which is currently 85–90% complete. This is an issue with many software products. A project is started by one or more programmers. If something happens to that person or group, it

> **There are decisions that every investor, developer, or owner must make many times during their careers, relating to whether they really want to see a project to completion or whether it just might be the wrong time or the wrong product.**

is very difficult to hand it to a new group. The new group will have to go over all the original code and figure out what was done, or just start over. I had to ask if I was willing to do this, or if I had different priorities.

> **In software development it is ideal to have at least two programmers working on a project, in case one leaves. It is difficult working with college students, because they are not sure where they would like to go after graduation. With the shortage of programmers and the competitive rates companies pay, a startup must have enough funding to offer a competitive rate.**

Do I think of BulletinCloud.com as being a success? If the development of a unique, powerful application that handles enough functionality to be useful is a success, then yes. Will it make any money? That seems unlikely, without dedicated support from a developer and myself. And yet, it was a success for me to choose which companies to invest my energies into. I picked the companies that had the best short-term potential. (BulletinCloud was more of a long-term investment, because of the need to complete the software and then do all the testing needed to prove it works well and has a strong potential for building a large user base.)

At this point the best option would be to find a developer or any entrepreneur who might want to own a company, finish the product, and market it. I am looking for these people as of summer 2018. This is a great opportunity for some ambitious developer who would want to be an owner in a product. There is still no product that has all the functionality built into BulletinCloud. It would work great as a bulletin board application for colleges, businesses, clubs, churches, etc.

> **Without a clear goal to finish a product, it will probably never be completed. There must be a goal and a commitment, or it will never be completed.**

It is difficult to be successful in a new venture without dedicating all of your energy (in this case, BulletinCloud was only a part-time venture). I possibly should have dropped one of my other interests to be able to invest more time in completing BulletinCloud, but at the time I was writing this book and was involved in other companies.

Chapter 13:
Denny the Muffin Man

Denny started his first business when he was only 13. He lived on a farm that grew strawberries. He started selling by walking around to neighbors, pulling his cart with boxes of strawberries. The last neighbor on his route told him that she would always purchase all the strawberries he had left. Being a smart businessman even at 13, Denny figured out that he could skip the walk and go directly to this last neighbor. Luckily for Denny this woman did not change her mind, or he would have had to build his business back again!

> It's never good practice to have only one customer. If anything ever happens to that relationship or that customer, your business could fail overnight.

Denny's entrepreneurial spirit didn't stop with strawberries. He went to the University of Pittsburgh and learned a lot about business acumen. Then he spent over a decade in corporate America. At this point Denny was working in sales. His employer allowed him to develop his own sales style, and by the early '90s he was earning three to four million in sales for his employer.

But like most entrepreneurs, working for someone else wasn't what Denny wanted. Around 1994 he heard there was a local coffee shop for sale. He called to put in an offer, but it had already been sold. A year later he went back to the shop and found out the new owners were not happy. They signed an agreement on a napkin to let Denny purchase the shop for $45,000.

Denny quit his job, knowing that his family could survive on his wife's paycheck until the shop was profitable. He never worried about whether he could make money (he just assumed he could). This confidence is important when going into business. Without the confidence, a new business owner might be too conservative and miss out on opportunities.

After purchasing the shop, Denny's workday lasted from 4 a.m. until 3 p.m. every day, six days a week. This was enough to keep the bakery shop running, but it wasn't enough for Denny's aggressive business goals.

He got involved in community service through his business. This was part of his marketing plan. Denny became well-known in the community as the bakery-owning Muffin Man. By being involved in evening and weekend events, he could spread the word about his shop, and people meeting Denny would want to stop by to say hello and eat.

The business had started with eight employees and grew to as many as 18. Only two or three were full time, which kept benefit costs down. Denny created the atmosphere to make people — employees and customers — feel good. The Muffin Man grossed a half million in sales, which made it a profitable business definitely beating the industry average.

Denny made enough to be happy. He had entertained the idea of franchising, but never did. This model was very successful at generating revenue and reputation, but it was also tiring. Denny eventually sold the Muffin Man. After 10 years, when Denny sold he made back eight times the initial investment.

During his 10 years owning the business, there was an instance when one of the ingredients for his muffins went up in price and Denny decided to try a less expensive different ingredient. What he found was that it changed the muffins just enough that people complained. He immediately went back to the original ingredient.

> **Never waiver from the quality of your product. When you don't see how you can afford to keep it up remember any compromise and your business might suffer. This is advice to take for any business.**

Denny was smart enough to know that it's better to make a little less profit and have consistently happy customers. Making more money per muffin but losing customers or reputation is not worth it. Denny's assessment of going into business for yourself is: "The thrill of the risk overcomes the stress." Over the years Denny has picked up a few properties and is now a landlord. He currently owns three buildings.

Chapter 14:
Tracking Highly Regulated Products

Mike started as a young kid picking up work and never seeming to get along with people of authority. He worked best as a loner and was not one for taking risks. But by the age of 15, Mike knew he was good at solving problems. He got a job installing point of sale (POS) systems for a company and helped to replace every POS terminal at Knoebels (a large local amusement park). At 17 Mike enlisted in the Air Force, but he received a medical discharge at just 19.

He went back to work at the same POS company and enrolled in college for computer information science. As a freshman, he became a network admin helping the college migrate from Novell to Microsoft active directory. The biggest problem with this education was that he was learning Cobol and Fortran, which were not going to get him a job with a future in the early 2000s.

When he graduated Mike was bored with his current job, which made him unhappy. He also butted heads with his managers, regularly. Mike always had a rocky employment road because of his tendency to argue.

Like many smart, stubborn people, Mike eventually asked, "Why not do it by myself," so he started an IT business and consulting company. He spent three years trying to get a customer (while working part time at another company to make ends meet). Eventually, he decided to look for another job and went to work for another IT company. Luckily for Mike, his wife had a good steady job with health benefits. She was behind him, always feeling that Mike would find his place in the business world.

After a few years of "normal" work, he decided to try again. This time he used social networking (the old-fashioned kind) to find customers. He spoke to potential customers face to face at bars, parties, and networking events, and he found a few who were eager to work with him. He did the work and still worked for a local company on the side.

For those of you who will own a company, try to always save a customer as long as they are worthwhile. It takes money and time to find a new customer. Customer retention is very important.

The company Mike worked for did not have a great reputation, and several clients fired the company. Mike picked up these customers outside of work, thinking it was not a conflict of interest because they fired the company.

This was the first time Mike had a plan and invested the energy to make a real go of his own company. He built a website. Then a local service-based company noticed Mike, and people began calling asking Mike's company to do work for larger companies in the area. A different local company called Mike and offered him a job on the spot. He agreed to a COO position and a salary, and he said he would transfer all service contracts from his own company to his new employer. Mike worked out the contract so he would still own the customers as well as leads generated through his own company.

> **Hiring an employee who wants to own their old customers and leads that are generated through them, is a like hiring an employee with one foot out the door. If you really want that person you are taking on a risk, that might not be worth it.**

For those of you considering hiring someone like Mike, a contract such as this raises red flags. You want someone who wants to work and stay with your company, not someone who already has one foot out the door. I would recommend having a clause that after a one-year anniversary, all customers would then be owned by the employer (special compensation could be paid for the sales to these older customers for a period of time). On the other hand, Mike did exactly what he should have by laying out his terms before taking a position.

Mike went to work and was able to reduce costs at the new company, growing revenue 40–60% during his next 18 months. He then asked for ownership of the company and was denied — and quit. He went back to his own company, with even more conviction that self-employment was the right path for him.

That is when Mike fully understood he needed to have his own company and that he needed to double-down efforts to make it a success. Since customer acquisition had been difficult for him in the past, he focused on establishing relationships with companies that could pass leads on to him. He became a Verizon premier partner and enterprise solutions provider. Verizon was looking for partners that forecast 2,000 units a year, but there was no penalty for not making this goal. Mike was smart enough to take the deal, and this kicked off lead generation by Verizon.

Why become a Verizon partner with the enterprise group? When you sign up and show a specific technical strength, Verizon corporate will give a lead to a partner who can potentially solve a customer's need.

They were referring lots of people, and one of the leads they received was for a transport company. Mike met with the potential customer who wanted to track the transportation of human organs and patients. The problem was they keep getting lost — and obviously this was a high-stakes problem!

Mike said he could arrange a tracking device that could include GPS and cellular support. He proposed this without actually having a solution, which meant he needed to start working on the solution immediately. He continued networking and took advantage of referrals to funding organizations and outside developers so that he could provide a strong demo. But he ran into a significant problem: shortly before presenting to the customer, the programming company he was using closed, and the software was not finished. He did not have the existing source code, either.

Mike had to make a critical decision. Would he give up or dig in and recommit to this product, customer, and presentation? He had grit. In the next seven days he got a platform spun up that did what was needed for a prototype, and he was able to demo it. His was the first company to take on GPS tracking of organs. Prior to Mike's solution, a report had been published saying that the tracking was not financially viable.

His biggest hurdle became apparent at a show. Potential customers needed proof that his young company, Novipod, was steadfast enough to be trusted to handle this complex task without going out of business. No one ever asked for revenue, they only looked at how long the company was around to see if they were reputable. The industry as a whole was skeptical.

Again, he demoed his product, using the relationship with Verizon to establish credibility even though his own company was young. Novipod developed a reseller agreement with the transport company, giving him an exclusive in this industry for organ transplants with Verizon. Verizon became a reseller of Novipod services and products.

Mike is much more comfortable working for himself. His software works with hundreds of pieces of equipment, using a common communication protocol. Success seems likely, but like most startups just having one or two customers and a proven solution isn't enough to guarantee profitability. Mike still relies to some extent on outside funding, though he hopes to turn the corner very soon. Since Novipod has a product that is scalable, it is more likely to succeed than a service-based company (that is limited by the number of employees).

Mike's story illustrates a few important lessons:

- Mike did not take the true plunge into being an entrepreneur until he realized that he needed to work for himself in order to be happy. That true motivation enabled him to put in the time and effort necessary to make a go of it as a startup. For a time, he put the business in front of everything and put himself into it completely.
- Mike realized that setting up relationships with vendors who can bring leads to him is extremely valuable; it is very difficult to do it all yourself.
- Mike also realized that sometimes there are many false starts before hitting on the right combination of product, customer, and luck to make a business work.
- Mike was fortunate to have a wife who was employed, which continued to give them money to live on.
- And finally, Mike protected himself throughout the process, negotiating strict deals with customers and employers. That allowed him to balance the growth of his own business with his other jobs while he was transitioning into full-time entrepreneurship.

Chapter 15:
Entrepreneurship in Video, Golf, and More

Thinking back, Kevin first exhibited grit working on his father's beef farm. Both parents had professions, and the farm was used to instill discipline in their kids. Dad was a lawyer and worked hard. Working hard, and pushing his kids, pleased him; he definitely encouraged his kids to use grit to be successful.

Kevin enjoyed making things from a young age. In high school he built rope courses and got youth groups, Boy Scout groups, and others to use the courses he'd created. When he got into programming, he immediately began considering ideas for products and companies he could start.

Initially, Kevin developed small games and was interested in graphical art. His first company was started with three other students when he was a freshman in college. Then he created a product to manage online textbook sales for college students. The product was free to use, and he received a 5% commission on each book purchased. This product had a nationwide rollout, expanding from school to school. Penn State became a customer, and Kevin was able to run this company until he was a senior. But there was not enough profit to make this a full-time job for Kevin.

He moved to Comcast to build products, and there he stepped into a difficult and instructive situation. Excite.com, an old email service, went through a transition, and it was necessary to move all of its customers over to Comcast within 60 days. When working with Comcast, Kevin was able share knowledge and to learn from other employees. The sharing of knowledge is one benefit of working with other smart people in a larger company.

Then Kevin left Comcast to create a company developing software that would plug into any LED sign for roads. It was like a content management system for signs: a modifiable package for different types of businesses like auto dealerships, gas stations, etc. The sign company was a success, but it couldn't grow as much as Kevin wanted. Digital signage is bigger in China, and Kevin felt he would have to move there to be truly successful. Since he didn't want to move to China, he decided to find something else.

When he'd been at Comcast, he had worked closely with Adobe. Jeremy Allaire, a leader at Adobe, had started a company called Brightcove. Jeremy and Kevin had a good relationship, and in 2004 Kevin joined Brightcove.

At this point, video on the Internet was just starting. Kevin recognized how important this technology would be. He worked like it was his own company, leading a small team and putting in long hours to develop video encode technology. They were in the right market at the right time: Brightcove eventually went public and Kevin made money from the deal.

Kevin left Brightcove in late 2006 to create oobgolf.com, a golf app that communicates and tracks scores and statistics, all free. He also started Naugle Group, a recruiting service that had a good network and made a commission for anyone recruiting through the company. Kevin had a partner who was a recruiter who became part owner in both companies.

Oobgolf grew its community to 100,000 golfers, first via a web service and then through an Apple app. At that point in time, a competitor had a product that owned 70–80% of the market. Due to changes in both companies' structure and how they each took advantage of Apple apps and hardware, Oobgolf was able to succeed as well.

A few years later, Kevin created a new startup known as Ponyup. Users could bet on anything against other people they knew. The money was escrowed for them to be paid to the winner. The business failed because it never got traction from consumers. It was not focused enough and closed the doors in late 2013.

> **If you are in a business and not enjoying yourself, either fix the problem or figure a way to sell or get out. Make sure to handle it professionally without burning any bridges, and try to make some money. Previous workers can become business assets in the future.**

Kevin then joined AirCare labs. This company took advantage of a legal change from the Affordable Care Act. Under the ACA, insurance payments to hospitals would decrease if people came back with the same problem. If more than 30% of heart attack patients came back within 30 days, then there was no payment to the hospital. The hospitals had to reduce re-admission rates. AirCare helped communication between outpatient and in-patient coordination. The system identified when a patient had a high risk of readmission. The app would ask the patient questions to know when it was important for a patient to talk to the doctor. This drastically cut down readmission.

AirCare had a successful pilot for a telephone system and an Android-based app. It also received a large federal grant and had two significant paying customers. However, Kevin realized that he did not want to do more work in the medical field. With high industry regulations, it can be very difficult to launch a product and have it adopted. The slow pace wasn't a good fit.

Kevin did some consulting and created a few minor apps while considering what to do next. A colleague from a previous company reached out about a concept called PlayImpossible. It was a consumer product: a ball with electronics that would communicate with apps for tracking/measurement. The product's designer had a proven track record; he was one of the main designers of the Fitbit. The CEO had been involved in other technology companies. And for the electronics portion of the product, he called on Kevin.

Kevin worked for PlayImpossible for free at first, deciding whether he wanted to commit. By the end of 2015, he had decided to join and lead the company through its first prototype.

PlayImpossible did not originally get much funding, and the owners were not paid. There were many problems getting the manufacturing of the product to work correctly. The communications for the ball had to be solid and very rugged. This proved to be quite a task for Kevin to figure out. Luckily the ball was being manufactured by Baden (the largest ball manufacturer in the U.S.). This became a joint effort to create a working ball that could talk to the phones.

Because Kevin and I had spent time throwing ideas off each other and helping each other when possible, he contacted me. He wanted my opinion about this project. He was already an owner in the company, earning his piece of the company through sweat equity (meaning he earned a share in the company by working and developing the hardware/software solution). Kevin explained the product then demoed it to me. Right away, I was sold. I understood the market, and the company already had many of the important pieces in place to get to the next stage.

Kevin explained that they were looking for investors. They currently only had a small amount invested. The three owners were putting in all their time for free and were looking for investors to subsidize the purchasing for electronic boards. They had a great partner set up for manufacturing the ball. I asked how much they were looking for and Kevin spelled out how much was needed now versus in the future.

By mid-2017 the manufacturing issues were resolved and by last quarter of 2017 the ball was being sold on Amazon and in some Target stores. Prior to Christmas, sales were good, and all the balls manufactured were sold. Sales did slow down after Christmas, just like for all toys. By spring of 2018, PlayImpossible worked out a deal with Apple to have the ball sold and demoed in all the Apple stores. This was a big deal and hopefully the start of a great relationship. By Christmas of 2018 the sales of PlayImpossible hit 22,000 units, which was on track.

The owners of PlayImpossible fall into that potentially successful mold by having the grit to make the company grow. The development, marketing, and other tasks get done, even if it means long hours, missed social engagements, and a passion to make the company successful.

Side Note: I thought this was a great idea. Because I was already involved in two other companies, I did the next best thing to trying to join up with the company: I invested as an early stage investor.

Why would I want to invest and get involved with a new company rather than start a new one?

- **PlayImpossible is poised to be a leader in a brand-new field: tying play activities to your phone or tablet (called Active-Play). Everyone loves their phones and tablets and wants to use them as much as they can. Adding physical activities and learning activities to the phone or tablet for children and young adults is something every parent would love.**

- **The technologies in this product yielded three provisional patents (or one patent with three parts).**

- **The experience and track record of the three partners was excellent.**

So, I offered to be an investor. I also offered to help in testing the product, coming up with new games, potentially helping to get new investors, and getting the product into new markets. I thought this would be a good fit since I already respected Kevin.

What would be the exit strategy for PlayImpossible? The exit strategy is an open question that all the investors are asking.

> **You need to exit if you think it either does not have a bright future or you are really not having fun. (Yes, fun is something many entrepreneurs have even when working 18 hours a day.)**

What all of Kevin's stories show is that Kevin is one of those serial entrepreneurs who adapt and learn enough to be successful in anything they try. It is important to note that none of the companies Kevin has owned or worked for would have been successful without very hard work and dedication. Still, not every business or deal will be profitable or fully successful even if you are very bright and want it to work.

A final lesson from Kevin's career is that networking is essential. Almost all of his ventures involved partnership with someone he had known through a previous business relationship. Having a strong network of contacts means that you can reach out to the right people when you need help — and that people will bring you opportunities that you're likely to find interesting.

> **Networking with people is a necessity for a successful entrepreneur. Relationships with other smart, creative people will enhance the chance of being successful.**

Chapter 16:
Complex Warehousing and Fulfillment Center

In the late '80s I worked with a company that exemplifies a classic business situation. Jim owned a fulfillment service, and he was selling some small-ticket items using magazine ads. His business was good, but it remained very small.

One day he was speaking with a friend who wanted to go into the beauty product business, which required warehousing and shipping solutions. This friend was limited by living in an apartment and working a full-time job: he couldn't stock inventory, create invoices, match them to orders, and essentially run the fulfillment side of his business while also managing the sales side and meeting obligations for his actual job.

Jim mentioned that he might be interested in handling his friend's problem, since he already had a warehouse. As is so often the case, what felt like a one-off opportunity for a friend developed into a new business model. The business of handling inventory, shipping, and billing for others seemed very promising, and Jim knew that he would need to grow his systems significantly to become a true fulfillment service for multiple businesses.

> **Changing an existing business can be very involved and have many similar traits to starting a new company. Decisions must be made to make sure you do not over-extend something that already works.**

This was a major pivot point. For Jim, expanding his business this way meant not just new software, but also a larger location and more employees, as well as time lost while automating his current inventory and invoicing systems. Mini-Byte had already created his single-user solution, so the ways that he decided to change and grow would require changes to our current solution.

Jim had to sit down, talk to everyone involved, examine his finances, and make a detailed plan. The warehouse landlord had to approve the renting of a larger space, the rack supplier had to be prepared to provide new racks, and the company needed to be working with an equipment company for a new lift. Jim collected quotes and determined that the overall plan was feasible, as long as he was willing to borrow money and work extremely long hours until the business was truly up and running. Then Jim and I sat down to redesign his inventory/invoicing system.

Most software solutions are designed for one company ordering inventory, receiving inventory, taking orders from customers, shipping, billing, and receiving funds. Jim needed a software solution that could handle all these functions for multiple companies on one system. The system also needed to handle all the orders for Jim's customer's customers. Each vendor Jim worked with had his or her own customers, inventory, billing, etc.

After a few meetings, specifications needed to be written and approved. Now Mini-Byte Software had to come up with a quote. For small-business owners, quotes need to be accurate, which is why truly understanding the scope of the modifications is key. This entire process was fun for Jim and me because we were learning so much about what needed to be completed to handle all aspects of the business prior to launching this new venture.

> **Enjoying business challenges is an important characteristic of successful entrepreneurs.**

For a service company like Mini-Byte, accurate quoting and explaining your quotes well is essential. In this case, I had to help Jim understand every complexity that the new software would have to accommodate:

- In a standard system there is one company doing billing. All the customers belong to that company, and all inventory, ordering, and invoices are just for that one company. The new system would need to handle multiple customer lists belonging to each new company, shipping its own products. This meant that inventory had to be managed for each company separately. When an order came in from a customer, everything including invoices needed to be associated with the correct company. When something was picked from the shelves and sorted for shipping and invoices, it all had to be matched to the correct company and correct customer. Then when the order was picked, it needed a shipping ticket and invoice for the customer from whichever company took the original order. When money was collected, it needed to go to the correct company, for the correct customer.
- If all this was not complicated enough, the system had to manage a billing system that could invoice each company for each order that was picked, shipped, and invoiced.
- Perhaps most importantly, the system had to be deeply reliable. If the computer or software system went down, all the companies

would stop shipping and invoicing, and their relationship with Jim would be significantly damaged. Everything had to be tested and tested, over and over again, before going live.

Quoting a system like this can be a disaster for a software development company. If a fixed price is given and the amount of time was calculated incorrectly, it could severely hurt the profitability of the software company. In a job such as this, it is recommended that the entire job be approved by someone in the company responsible for getting projects done profitably and on time. Most software companies will not give a fixed quote because it is so difficult. Then there is always the issue of scope creep. Many times, a design that is agreed upon changes as the work is carried out. This can be caused by a number of factors, most often a failure to account for specific needs up front, or the customer deciding that he or she needs additional functionality. Pushing back against scope creep is essential to keeping a service company profitable.

Jim was willing to spend the time that it took to achieve the solution. He knew it would give his company an edge over his competition and the ability to offer high technology to other small companies. This was the start of a company that had the ability to grow significantly within a few years. Mini-Byte had signed a contract with Jim that the software would not be sold to any companies within a 75-mile radius. This protected Jim from direct local competition. But Mini-Byte still had the chance to sell the software to other companies outside of that radius, and since it was such a unique solution Mini-Byte wanted to be able to resell. Since Jim was paying for all the development, he really wanted it to be exclusive. We came to terms by agreeing that Jim would get a commission every time the software was sold to a potential customer for the first 18 months after it was up and running. Jim would also act as a reference for the software. Mini-Byte software retained complete ownership.

Here is where both companies needed to be careful. For Jim, once he signed, he would not be able to claim any ownership or control of the software after 18 months. So it was important that he build his business within two years so that customers would pick his company, even if others adopted a similar system. For Mini-Byte, we had to make sure that our profit from the deal with Jim was enough to carry us even if we could not sell locally, and we had to make sure that we protected our intellectual property in the long run.

Ultimately, this deal was a win/win. Both companies did well, and Mini-Byte sold the software many times over. Ultimately, a very powerful automated warehousing system was developed starting with the core inventory system. The warehouse product was sophisticated enough to be split off from Mini-Byte software and sold to one of the largest warehouse customers in New Jersey (which by that time was changing direction).

What can you get out of this story? If you create a solution for a specific industry, there is a good chance that a business can develop around it. The end game in this case was making an extra profit selling the rights to the entire solution. It is very important to quote accurately and watch for scope creep.

Conclusion:

Many of the lessons of entrepreneurship are best learned when you experience them personally. Through his or her career, each entrepreneur will accumulate a wealth of knowledge about business scenarios. Reading stories like the ones contained in this book can help you learn how to handle business situations as well as the risks and possibilities you should consider. I also suggest that any aspiring entrepreneur work with a mentor to discuss ideas, choices, and plans. Learn from real-life examples and advice to understand what we mean when we say, "Oh boy, that entrepreneur has grit."

I've written this book to collect many of my business insights in one place. For those who want to cut straight to the chase, I've summarized the most important business lessons here.

DO YOU HAVE WHAT IT TAKES?

Not everyone is cut out to be an entrepreneur, and that's okay. Recognizing your limitations early on is much better than recognizing them once you've invested significant time and money into a business. Successful entrepreneurs are:

- Willing to work hard, for long hours
- Able to listen and take advice
- Visionary about their ideas, products, market, and strategies
- Able to enjoy their work
- Passionate enough to push on
- Experts in their field
- Constantly coming up with new ideas
- Willing to learn from others
- Thick-skinned and able to take criticism

Your attitude will guide you through all the work ahead. It will also shape the environment for others who will be working with or for you.

IS YOUR IDEA MARKETABLE AND REALISTIC?

Creating a new company and potentially a new product or service is not easy. If it were easy, everyone would do it. If your product was an obvious, guaranteed success, there's a very good chance someone would have already done it. Because of this, you need to honestly evaluate your idea, taking a user's point of view and determining:

- Who needs your product or service, and how valuable is it to them?
- Is that value high enough for your company to be profitable?
- What solutions would you be competing against, and in what ways is yours better/worse?
- What are your true costs (manufacturing, overhead, shipping, etc.) in providing your product or service, and what profit margin could that leave you with?

Ultimately, we all want to consider our ideas as awesome solutions. You need that faith in yourself to be successful. But you also need to realistically examine the market and be able to admit when a product or idea is not a fit. Being honest in this way from the beginning will let you focus your energy on your best ideas.

WHO ELSE IS INVOLVED IN YOUR COMPANY?

Many people decide to start their own businesses because they don't want to work for someone else. They want to "be their own boss." It's not quite as simple as that, though.

You need to keep the customers satisfied and understand their needs. Of course, you can quit a customer, but that's a serious decision. It means less income. In other words, you can never really get away from working for someone. As an entrepreneur, you won't have one boss—you'll have lots of bosses. Every customer is your boss, especially if you are in a service business.

You can never get away from working with others. Unless you are truly the only person in charge of your business, you need to consider how to work carefully with employees and potential partners. Partners are a particularly difficult addition. Having a partner is like getting married — in fact, you'll likely spend more time with a business partner than you do with your spouse.

From the beginning, make sure you have a way to get a "divorce" if things don't work out. Most partnerships do not last forever, and virtually all breakups are messy and expensive. This is especially important to consider if the partner is a family member. You want to arrange a way to separate your business relationship amicably so that you can maintain a friendship.

Before beginning to work with a partner, ensure that they have morals, work habits and financial values that match your own. Often, partners should receive no paycheck in the early days of a startup. (Cash needs to be focused on overhead and the processes to get your business up and running.)

Employees are easier to consider than partners, but they are still an important and complicated part of any business. When hiring, make sure that each individual brings specific skills the company needs. You may need technical, financial, marketing, or engineering skills to complement your own. Keep in mind that employees, partners, and all of the other people involved in your business bring risk and variability into your world. You need to balance that with the certainty that they also bring skills and work ethic that will help move you toward success.

WHAT SHOULD YOU EXPECT IN EARLY DAYS AS A STARTUP?

A startup's early days are full of stress about money, hard work, and many late nights. It can be a tumultuous and risky time, which is why it's so important to evaluate whether you have the mindset to be successful as an entrepreneur.

All startups require a big investment of time. This means that you will need your friends' and family's emotional support — and perhaps financial support — to see you through the early stages. If you have a spouse, partner, or children who do not want to support you in this way, you will become frustrated and are likely to fail.

Of course, you have to consider practicalities like location, too. Most entrepreneurs start out in a home office, garage, or some other inexpensive location. Usually everyone is on a strict budget. Unless you are opening a retail outlet, warehouse, repair shop, or another type of business that needs a specific location, a home office or really small office might work and be a good way to save money in early days. Usually most companies hire one or two people at a time, which means you can upgrade and move to larger facilities as you grow. Whenever possible use furniture and equipment that you or someone you know already owns. Keep costs down. You don't need a fancy office when starting out. You need to save money for growing the business.

HOW SHOULD YOU ORGANIZE YOUR FINANCES?

Many startups fail during the first year because of a lack of finances. It is important to start with enough saved to last a year without any income from the business. If your spouse works, live on that income. If you still work and this new business is a side venture, you might be more financially stable. Sometimes this is a smart idea; you can continue working while developing the ideas for the new company or product. But you will reach a point where the business will need you full time to get to the next level. It's important to consider when you will make that switch.

While forming the company, keep its finances separate from your personal accounts. Go through the process to officially form a corporation or an LLC. This protects your personal money and helps with taxes. Consider taking out liability insurance to cover any incidents that might occur.

> **Always play by the rules when paying taxes. There are many legal loopholes that an accountant will know about that are totally legitimate. Don't ever do anything that might bring on an audit.**

It's worth asking for professional help when you're organizing your business's finances, since there are often complicated tax implications. Consider seeing an accountant or your local SBDC. And of course, try finding a mentor who has experience growing a business.

Business loans are another beast. It is difficult to set up a line of credit for a new company. Usually, you need to put up collateral and build a line of credit or take out a loan. But as a new company, you will personally be responsible for the loan. Once your company is established and you have a proven track record, things become easier. There are potentially state and local organizations that might offer a loan to the business (with the idea that you will be hiring employees and giving back to the community).

If you are very confident that your idea is a winner, talk to family members. Just remember that you really need to be committed before asking friends or family members for money. If you fail, quit early, or don't put any of your own finances into play; you can destroy a family relationship or a friendship.

HOW DO YOU LET THE WORLD KNOW ABOUT YOUR BUSINESS?

A website is your first avenue for explaining what your company has to offer. This can be a very expensive proposition. Just like a startup may begin in a home office before moving to an expensive location, your website can start as a homemade endeavor. Try creating a website yourself, or with someone who has creative experience, using a service like Wix or Weebly whose easy templates make this possible. Using these sites you can create retail environments, sell products, take credit cards, or just explain what your company does. You can include videos and graphics. It's crucial that any site created today is responsive, meaning that it works on cellphones and tablets (not just desktop computers). As your business succeeds you will move to a larger, more complex and professional website. But a homemade site — as long as it looks polished — can be a good way to establish a web presence without undue costs. Make sure that you have friends, relatives, or business partners read and edit every page on the website. Errors do not instill confidence in potential customers.

As you create your site, consider and focus on your audience and the primary call to action that you want to provide. If you want someone to "buy now," ensure that that experience is easy, seamless, and supported by the entire site. Instead, you may want someone to call you, sign up for a newsletter, or otherwise express interest. Keeping your audience and call to action in mind will significantly help your website support your business goals.

It's also important to consider what role, if any, social media and digital marketing plays in your world. There are many platforms to get your name out ranging from blogs, Facebook, and Twitter to Google AdWords, LinkedIn campaigns, and more. All involve some cost in terms of time and money. You need to be selective about which to invest in. Additionally, you need to consider your calls to action and goals for these platforms. If someone shows up ready to buy, is your product ready and do you have inventory?

Finally, here are a few of my favorite general pieces of advice for entrepreneurs. This is a list to return to over and over again, when you're feeling discouraged or looking for some guidance:

- The big picture is important, but details you've ignored could kill your product. Pay close attention.
- Taking risks and getting out of your comfort zone is necessary. Remember that you have not failed, you have just found 1,000 ways that don't work.
- Luck is a part of every successful business. It's also true that the harder and smarter you work, the luckier you become!
- Be persistent. When you run into problems, try dissecting the situation or looking at it from another point of view to find a solution. If you are ready to quit, remember the old proverb: "The

temptation to quit will be greatest just before you are about to succeed."

- Never stop learning. Many industries change quickly, and you must stay educated to stay ahead of your competition.
- Focus on the future, not the past. Learn from your mistakes; the greatest failure is not to try.
- Pay attention to your competitors all the time. They might be moving forward and making improvements that you're not aware of.
- As someone considering entrepreneurship, you already have passion. Half of what separates the successful entrepreneur from the non-successful is pure grit.

Best of luck on your entrepreneurial journey.

Glossary:

Accounts Receivable (A/R) – Money due to a business from clients for services provided or products delivered.

Affiliate – Someone who promotes your product and will only earn a commission if sales are made by their affiliate source.

Angel Investor – A private individual or group that invests in a business.

B2B Sales – Marketing your products and services to other businesses rather than individual consumers.

Collateral – Anything of value that can be pledged against a loan.

Competitive Landscape – A business analysis that identifies direct and indirect competitors.

Copyright – A form of intellectual property law that protects original works of authorship including literary, dramatic, musical, and artistic works, such as poetry, novels, movies, songs, computer software, and architecture.

CRM – Customer relationship management (CRM) is a term that refers to practices, strategies and technologies that companies use to manage and analyze customer interactions and data

dBase - One of the first database management systems for microcomputers (and the most successful in its day).

Design Patent – Legal protection for a unique ornamental design in your product.

Empowerment Zone (Similar to KIZ) - Economically distressed communities designated by government for aid that offers State or Federal tax breaks. This aid is intended primarily to lift the communities out of poverty by stimulating business enterprise and creating jobs.

EntreMetric – An online assessment for measuring the Entrepreneurial Mindset.

Entrepreneurship – The process of designing, launching, and running a new business, which is often initially a small business.

Exit Strategy – An exit strategy is a plan for how to handle the company in the future which might include exiting the business while it is still a viable entity. Some possible options are: Merger & Acquisition (M&A), Initial Public Offering (IPO), Sell to a friendly individual, find someone to run the company and keep the profits, Liquidation and close

Grit – The quality of perseverance, courage, resolve, and risk tolerance; strength of character.

Intellectual Property (IP) – A nontangible property such as a patent or trade secret to which one has legal rights.

Just in Time (JIT) Inventory - An inventory strategy to increase efficiency and decrease waste by receiving goods only as needed for the production process, which reduces inventory costs. JIT inventory management is more appealing for retailers, as it allows them to sell a product before buying it, then purchase the item from a third party and have it shipped directly to the customer.

KIZ - Keystone Innovation Zone (KIZ) Tax Credit Program_- An incentive program that provides tax credits to for-profit companies less than eight years old operating within specific targeted industries within the boundaries of a Keystone Innovation Zone (available in Pennsylvania).

Limited Liability Company (LLC) – A limited liability company is a corporate structure whereby the members of the company are not personally liable for the company's debt or liabilities. Limited liability companies are hybrid entities that combine the characteristics of a corporation and a partnership or sole proprietorship.

NASA – National Aeronautics and Space Administration - Is an independent agency of the United States Federal Government responsible for the civilian space program, as well as aeronautics and aerospace research.

Patent - A form of intellectual property giving its owner the right to exclude others from making, using, selling, and importing an invention for a limited period of time.

Phantom Stock Options – A contractual agreement between a corporation and recipients of phantom shares that bestows upon the grantee the right to a cash payment at a designated time or in association with a designated event in the future

PlayImpossible - The Play Impossible Gameball is an active gaming system that brings the digital action indoors and outdoors with ten free connected games you can play on cell phones, tablets, computers or Apple TV.

Preferred Stock – A stock that entitles the holder to a fixed dividend, who payment takes priority over that of common-stock dividends.

Prototype – A first, typical, or preliminary model of a product.

S Corporation – A special structure of business ownership by which the business is able to avoid double taxation because it is not required to pay corporate income tax on the profits of the company.

Santa Cruz Operation – The Santa Cruz Operation, Inc. (SCO) became a leader in providing Unix operating systems in the 1980s and 1990s. It was very popular with VARs for installing Intel based multiuser business applications.

Scope Creep – Refers to changes, continuous, or uncontrolled growth in a project's scope at any point after the project begins. This can occur when the scope of a project is not properly defined, documented, or controlled.

Sole Proprietorship – A person who owns a business and is personally responsible for its debts.

Trademark – The name, logo or slogan that identifies a business.

Trade Name – The name a company uses to do business.

Unix - A family of multitasking, multiuser computer operating systems that derives from the original AT&T Unix. SCO purchased the version of Unix for the Intel processor.

VAR – Value Added Reseller - These are companies that sell something to enhance a product they are reselling. The added value could be a physical or service enhancement.

Xenix – A version of the Unix operating system for various microcomputer platforms, licensed by Microsoft from AT&T in the late 1970s. SCO later acquired exclusive rights to the software and eventually replaced it with SCO UNIX.

ABOUT THE AUTHOR

I hope to leave a good footprint by helping others find success and being a good role model.

The most important things in my life have been done with love and passion. This passion gives me my energy and the love is a reason to exist. By using your mind you can overcome many obstacles, whether physical or emotional. This is how I have managed through life's good and bad times. When I was younger I was consumed by gymnastics. When an injury caused me to stop, my passion became cars (and racing). During my first dozen years as a professional I was a teacher both in school and as a coach. In 1981 I found that with the aid of computers and graphics I was able to use my imagination to create simulations of the world around us. I started as a computer programmer and systems consultant for businesses in 1981. During the next 35 years, the businesses included networking, security, small business applications, animations, software applications, inventing new solutions to existing problems, running and owning businesses, consulting and mentoring. This was fun and a lot of work.

I have owned numerous technology-based companies, created software applications, and companies. In 2008 I decided to start volunteering to help startup companies including local businesses and student startups giving technology and business advice.

My latest adventure was to start a new company manufacturing a device to enable people with injuries or disabilities get out of bed without the use of their arms (www.footanchor.com). This has been another great learning opportunity and will give me the chance to donate 10% of our inventory to those in need who cannot afford assistance.

I feel as though I have been blessed to have wonderful people in my life that support and love me, and I am proud to be able to support and love others around me.

www.ingramcontent.com/pod-product-compliance
Lightning Source LLC
Chambersburg PA
CBHW071134050326
40690CB00008B/1460